THE LINES
THAT MAKE US

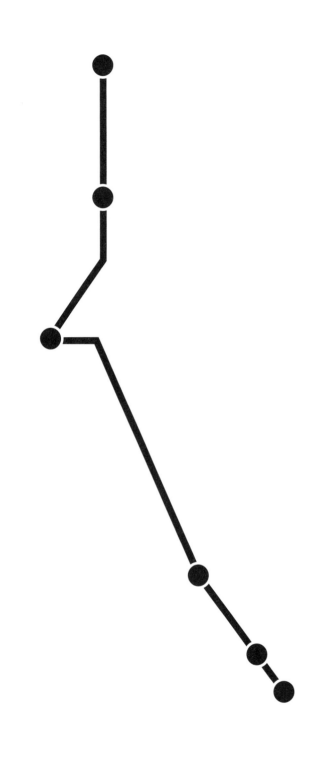

THE LINES THAT MAKE US

Stories from Nathan's Bus

Stories and photos by
Nathan Vass

Introduction by Paul Constant

Chin Music Press
Seattle, Washington

Contents

Preface

How I Write the Stories, and Why

I used to have a great fear of being in social situations where everyone knew everyone else, but I didn't know anybody. I forget the number of events I didn't attend to avoid this circumstance, and I also forget exactly when I started to find the experience strangely enjoyable. Probably when I began noticing there was usually someone who recognized me from bus-land, or art-world, or both. It's a little scary, going alone, but you're free to roam about as you wish, without strings, engaging as much or as little as you please. If the folks present are friendly, then all the better.

In 2012 I was invited to just such an event—an art show featuring work by the boyfriend of a passenger. Virginia was a grad student and regular rider on the 4 whom I'd driven home for—months? Years? I can't quite recall. Long enough for our brief interactions to slowly build into friendship, a point of connection of which was that her boyfriend, also named Nathan, was a photographer, like me.

My blog exists because I chose to go to Nate's photography event at Theo Chocolate in June 2012. It exists because Virginia was kind enough to extend the invite, and because I was able to get over my mild nervousness about going to an event where I would barely know anyone. It exists most potently because of a long conversation I got into with three delightful young women. One was a photographer; another had a background in medicine; the third owned an interior design company.

I had come directly from work, still wearing my little Metro cardigan, and after we discussed bus-land, they broached the idea of a blog. I stood there and tried to come up with excuses to justify not doing so. It sounds like a lot of work. It involves large amounts of time documenting life instead of living it. It means sitting in front of computers regularly, which I don't care for. The moments with the passengers are private and special, and writing about them would dilute their power. No one's going to be interested, because the events are positive. The events are too small—things like eye contact or fist bumps can't be interesting as focal points for stories... or can they?

How great that they correctly called me out for being lazy and making a bunch of lame excuses. "Just try it," they said, brightly. "People love stories."

The conversation was valuable enough that I became late for where I was going afterward—something friends know I'm loathe to do—but it was so utterly worth it. This whole enterprise might not exist otherwise. "You need to write about these stories," the women insisted. "You need to share them. People need to hear them, and they'll love them."

You'll notice a lot of dialogue in the stories. I want you to know that it is, to the best of my ability and memory, completely accurate. I have a great fascination with spoken language, and I love capturing its nuances and specifics. The starts and restarts, the repetition, the interruptions—quite different from much fictional dialogue, wherein characters patiently wait for each other to finish talking and express complete thoughts in organized, structured bursts of brilliance.

The linguistic enthusiasts among you will perhaps know that the Nixon tapes are the *largest existing document of the same people talking*. Think about that for a moment. It's a conversational gold mine. The resulting transcripts are invaluable examples of what spoken interactions actually look like on paper. The 800-page brick of a publication, *The Nixon Tapes*, culled from 3,000 hours of back-

Nathan Vass

room dealings and private conversations, focuses mostly on early-term material (we've all heard the Watergate tapes). Aside from the obvious historical value and disturbing Shakespearean undertones (perhaps overtones is more like it), the transcripts are revelatory in their unadorned depiction of human speech.

You realize people don't talk in paragraphs, let alone complete sentences. Page after page goes by of oddly rhythmic, staccato interruptions and roundabout developments of thoughts, like intercutting storyline threads in a Robert Altman movie. The subject comes to light only glancingly, gradually, a sum revealed only by taking it all in. It's a beautiful dance of sorts, the type we all engage in every day.

It is this fascination which compels me to document so many bus conversations in such detail, as honestly as possible. People reveal volumes of themselves in how they choose to phrase things, and in how thoughts emerge through the progression of two people interacting. I'll scribble down everything on transfers or paper towels as soon as it's safe to do so. I can fill in context later; at the outset all I care about is getting down the actual words. Keywords come first, quickly followed by word choice and structural details. When you do this enough times, your recall develops and remembering the idiosyncrasies of speech becomes an ingrained habit. Generally I start with the last (most recent) sentence of an exchange and work my way back through the conversation from there.

However, I can't get it all down every time. Many's the time when the conversation was so compelling—but so fast—that retaining it all was simply impossible. I'd sit there at a red light, thinking, What just happened? If I can't remember a conversation with confidence, it doesn't go on the blog. After all, if it isn't truthful, what's the point of telling it? For that reason, the stories generally involve only one other conversant and find a certain natural limit in length; after a certain point I just can't remember everything. As well, contemporary urban life is, as they say, R-rated; these stories are presented in their original and unexpurgated form. In my view, a truthful story has more value than a diluted one. I hope this is not offensive.

Even before the blog existed I would write little notes on transfers, in a journal, on napkins, strictly so I could remember the moments for myself. The first time I ever did so was when a teenage boy got off my (now long-extinct) 253 at Bellevue Transit Center. He was a Pacific Northwest teenager with an oversized button-up plaid shirt and skater shoes, and he thanked me with enthusiastic presence before removing his BMX bicycle.

You knew he'd never seen a driver near his age before (I was twenty-one at the time), and likely hadn't run into one with my put-all-of-yourself-out-there approach. The transfer note is long lost and I forget his exact words all these years later, but I can still see his attitude. In his keen ardor you felt the rising spirit of new possibilities, the beat of new horizons. Kids know how big the world can be. You *can* conflate coolness and kindness, high functioning and inclusiveness. He wheeled back and forth across the street, not ready to leave my sight, too excited by the new understandings forming in his head—insights on a summer afternoon, new ways we as young people can be. I was as energized by his unconcealed verve as he was by mine. He waited til the light turned green, and I started to drive out.

Me, tossing an upward nod his way, big wave, and he's grinning wide as he returns the gesture. Our generation.

These are the little births I treasure. I hope you enjoy reading them.

Nathan Vass

Introduction

Paul Constant

Since June of 2012, Nathan Vass has been blogging about his experiences as a driver for King County Metro. On his blog, *The View from Nathan's Bus*, he writes candidly about what he sees as a driver on the 7 line through Rainier Valley, which is commonly stereotyped as the city's most infamous route.

Operating a bus gives you a front row seat to the very best and worst of humanity. Vass witnesses surprising generosity and bitter conflicts on his daily trips, and he records it all. In five years on his blog, he's published posts about race and gender roles, and the changing face of Seattle, and art, and feces, and pretty much everything else you'll find on public transportation.

I had arranged to meet Vass for the first time at a coffee shop downtown for an interview. At first, I walked right past him. I failed to immediately recognize Vass for two reasons: first, he looks too young to drive a bus (he's a very youthful 32); and second, he was staring so intently at the paintings coffee shop employees were in the process of hanging that I assumed he was the artist. (Vass is a photographer and filmmaker in his spare time, currently working on his ninth feature.) In person, Vass is well read and deeply thoughtful; he keeps a journal by his side and takes notes whenever an idea occurs to him.

The name of his blog—particularly the "View" in *The View from Nathan's Bus*—is no accident; there's a reason why it's not *Over-*

heard on Nathan's Bus. Vass really *looks* at things—he notices fine details and takes in context and nuance. While many people wander the city in a daze, Vass doesn't miss a thing. In the middle of an answer, he stops and points out one of his regular riders, who just happens to be passing by across the street. He knows his name and what his days are like.

When Vass started driving for Metro in 2007, he says he was "resistant to the idea" of writing about his job because "I felt that we live in a time where documenting life is given priority over experiencing life, and I didn't want to fall into that." More than that, "These moments on the bus are quite special, but they're also private and precious—and perhaps I would be interfering with their preciousness by writing about them." He notes that memoirists often find their memories to be "shifted and reframed by what they've written" after converting their lives to "narrative form."

Ultimately, Vass says, his friends convinced him to share his stories with the world. He also thought that perhaps he could be a counter to the horrible news people encounter every day, that he could make his blog a space "for people who want to read about all the great things that are happening in this life, especially the subtle, everyday, beautiful things that I think a lot of us notice but don't talk about."

Vass had actually been writing about his route for years. During his breaks, he would write down noteworthy moments on the backs of bus transfers. He still remembers the first note, which was about "the look on this boy's face as he took off the bicycle from the front" of the bus—a look of "excitement and respect" and "vitality."

But when he started blogging, Vass realized it takes a lot more work to write a blog post than it does to scribble a note on a bus transfer. Vass says that on almost every post he writes, "The last paragraph or the last sentence—you can read that and know that I spent 45 minutes staring at the computer screen, figuring out how to write that." Vass often carries a printout draft of an upcoming post on him, and during breaks on his route he'll edit the piece with pen on paper. (He's an analog guy who shoots on film and prefers to listen to music on vinyl.)

The blog will continue for the foreseeable future. If anything, Vass has too many experiences to share. He's got plenty of notes written out on transfers "that seem like they'll make pretty good blog posts, but then they get tossed by the wayside because other things happen that are more interesting. And there's always more things."

But isn't blogging supposed to be dead as a platform for writing? Vass scoffs at the idea. When he's writing posts, they'll often "run longer than I think they will, and I discover they're actually about more than one thing. And I love that the blog allows for that space." He resists the brevity of Twitter and Facebook: "People are complex, and we can't address that complexity using only the most simplest and reductive of communicative forms. I think that's why books still persist, because we need that."

Vass admits that when he started out he was "apprehensive" about his bosses and coworkers reading his blog. And they definitely do read it: "There's a person in the HR department at Metro who's required to read everything I write," he says. But that HR staffer "shared with me that she's grown to look forward" to new posts, and that they give "the administrative staff at Metro an armchair perspective of what it's like to be on the street." Some of Vass's posts are used as training materials for new bus drivers, and he's been asked to speak to new classes. He believes that the administration likes that his blog "underlines the fact that this is a customer service gig. We're not driving around potatoes here."

Ask Vass for his influences and you'll get an impressive list in response: Tolstoy, Van Gogh's letters. But so far as literary influence goes, "The first name that flashes to mind is Don DeLillo." Vass loves DeLillo's obsession with and respect for the rhythm of the language: "The English language is large enough that you can [substitute] any word for another word for the sake of rhythm. And he's very meticulous about that. That's something that I try in my own very small way to emulate."

Over time, his blog has developed deeper rhythms and a novelistic understanding of time. Characters recur, and Vass grows to know his riders more and watch kids on his route grow up. It's a complex story of life in the city, and that booklike feeling is no accident.

But in the end, writing the blog is its own reward. Vass wants more than anything "to inspire a sense of hope and belief in other people—not just to make them feel better, but to make them think that, 'Okay, the world is a good place. Humans are good people.'" Does Vass really believe in the goodness of the human race? "I actually don't think it matters if that's true or not, but I think it does matter if people *think* it is. Because if they *think* the world's a good place, if they *think* people are great, then they'll be inspired to work hard at making that become closer to reality."

In the end, Vass says, as a bus driver and a photographer and a filmmaker and a writer, "I want to remind folks that you can contribute."

THE LINES THAT MAKE US

He didn't want to shoot stuff. He just wanted to dance.

INDEPEN-DANCE

7/5/2017

I don't have the ear to discern between the sound of certain fire-crackers and the sound of gunshots. Some of my passengers do, though, and plenty of both were being fired off this Tuesday past in Rainier Valley. That may be enjoyable for others, but speaking for myself, I wouldn't call it pleasant. I'm less than thrilled by it. So much of my writing is in some way an appreciation of Seattle's most underserved and crime-ridden neighborhoods, and regular readers know I have a real ardor for the Valley. I'm there often enough to consider it a second home, and know more people there than in my own neighborhood.

However.

The sound of guns, especially automatic weapons fire, does not bring me joy. The mixture of alcohol, weapons, explosives... it's no environment to do much of anything in, and definitely not to drive an electric bus connected to 750 volts of overhead trolley wire. As an older passenger said, "Those bullets come down, too!"

The bottom two-thirds of Rainier was an unending cavalcade of pops, booms, and crackles—clusters and aberrations in the soundscape, a celebration not of an event, not history, certainly not the founding of a country, but the act of celebrating itself. Understand, reader, how far a cry this is from the choreographed and legitimately wonderful spectacle North Seattle gets to witness at Gas Works Park. These scattered potshots and the bullets between them were never big enough to be beautiful, never elaborate enough to provoke awe. The odor of burnt flame and aggression, acrid, not quite right; sparkles booming in your periphery, up above but also in the dank side alleys, glimpses of undercontrolled blazes where you normally see children and forgotten furniture.

What will I remember of this July 4th, other than the sensation of having survived a battle upon making it out of the Valley, and entering into another upon going back down?

I'll remember the face of an East African man, appropriately inebriated for the holiday but confused. It was my second time seeing him that day, and this time around he was immaculately attired. Look at that crisp royal blue three piece, tailored; offset burgundy tie set against a white dress shirt, with matching white handkerchief peeking out of the breast pocket, just so; coiffed hair and jet-black shoes, shined so slick I could almost see myself in the reflection.

"My brother," he said, after I congratulated him on how sharp he looked. "My brother, what's going on, I don't understand. This holiday, what does it mean? What does it mean to you?"

"Well, we never celebrated it growing up. Korean household—"

"Okay okay, but no, but what does it mean to them?"

"Well, it's celebrating the, the beginning of the country—"

"The flag. Crossing the river."

"Yeah the flag, yeah—"

"It's a holiday, people should be out having good time, going to the club! Everything is closed! The Esquire, Royal Room... why people want to blow stuff up, fire their guns? I came to get away from that bullshit. These motherfuckers don't know. What happened

Nathan Vass

to people want to dance? It's a holiday! They should dance and be happy! I got all dressed up like this to go out!"

He didn't want to shoot stuff. He just wanted to dance.

Maybe one day we all will.

Homelessness is not a permanent state, and he was brand new at it.

FIRST DAY OF SCHOOL

7/29/2016

"Talkin' 'bout down there by the courthouse?"

I was trying to clarify the situation. He was asking directions.

"I don't know," he replied, struggling to stay upright, clutching his cane for dear life. I'm sure he was able-bodied once, in his younger days. "It's my first time doin' this."

He was an older African-American gentleman asking for the Downtown Emergency Service Center (DESC). Homelessness is not a permanent state, and he was brand new at it. All the chaos on the sidewalk was utterly foreign to him, and he, a frail and elderly disabled man, tried not to show his fear.

It's a zoo out here, I thought, surveying the mayhem. Figures lay draped about the cement in various states of consciousness. Some stared straight ahead. Others raged, lashing out, trying their hardest not to be invisible. Each has a mother. Can't tell if that's alcohol or urine or both, sizzling on the hot pavement, sticky. Hands over there shaking, worlds in the corner of an eye; secrets passing in broad daylight. Band aid after band aid after band aid, until we forget the names of our original problems.

I caught a woman peering with childlike confusion at the well-to-do working folk passing by, as if wondering: How is it that only some of us have to live out the worst consequences of our circumstances, our decisions?

Reader, I have to confess I love these people. They are more rude, but they are also more polite. The spectrum's just wider. All class groups act out intolerable behaviors, and the homeless are no exception; what moves me is the degree to which kindness and respect resonate with those who know what it is to be in the trenches. The short end of the stick, whether deserved or otherwise, is no great place to be. Being avoided, ignored, ostracized... acknowledgment cuts through all that, and has the power to remind us there are still good people about.

But all that is only my perspective. Third and James is a place I drive through nightly, containing people I know who like me. Great. For our elderly friend with the cane, diving in in a way I don't have to, the scene definitely didn't read as a collection of acquaintances and friends. It was a Boschian carnival of depraved bedlam. It was all new, the deep end of the pool of life, new and strange and dense with horror. Places seem larger when they're terrifying. His reedy voice shook as much as his unsteady cane, his corduroy orange jacket and fedora slightly too elegant—not what you wear to your first day of school, as it were.

"Be safe today," I said.

"Tonight!" he corrected.

"Tonight! Right on. Well, I'll be lookin' for ya. I'm out here all night too."

"Right on, man!"

"It'll be you and me!"

"I'll be lookin' for you too!"

The exchange was just the friendly push he needed. Oh, reader, listen to that beautiful boost of verve in his final line! Especially as compared to his trepidation just minutes before. He wasn't alone.

We're all in this together, he now recalled, we fellow humans, working it out, doing our best at this strange and crazy and nigh-impossible task we all share:

The act of living life.

Tragedy and comedy rub shoulders in such strange proximity.

THE CIRCLE OF SPELLING AND LIFE

6/5/2016

Bashi's talking to somebody next to him. "I would appreciate... I would appreciate it, to slumber. Not even sleep. Slumber. You—"

"Slumber?"

"Slumber means sleep."

"I know."

"S, L, U, M, B, E, R." At this point he calls out to me. "Hey Nathan! How you read it, S, L, U, M, B, E, R?"

Rest breaks were tight today due to a protest incident downtown. I used my five minute layover for stretching and the bathroom, and was then eating my sandwich in service. My philosophy: Take your break *while driving the route*. That way you're guaranteed a break! Anything else is gravy. Drive at twenty-five miles an hour, say hi to the people, and enjoy yourself. Life is short.

Yes, I did once drive from Rainier to the U-District with seaweed salad and chopsticks in one hand... though there's hardly enough red lights along that distance to get a proper meal in! The Rainier

Avenue kids looked at me askance. I like to think the chopsticks added a touch of class.

"Slumber," I said, in between mouthfuls. "It's like sleeping."

"Slumber."

"Like tired, yeah."

"Slumber. Hey what about... flabber-gast?"

"That's like very surprised."

"Oh, yeah!"

"Man, you're good!" we both said, incredibly, at precisely the same time.

"You're *good*, smart!"

"*You're* very smart!" I said.

"Flabbergast. I was flabbergasted." Bashi was well dressed, as he always is, and only slightly intoxicated today. He's a father, and tested out the word in a sentence, as I imagine he does when teaching new words to his children. "I was flabbergasted to see Mr. Donald Trump is leading the Republican party."

"I am flabbergasted too!" I laughed. To the incoming crowd at Edmunds, I exclaimed, "Hello everybody!"

"Man Nathan, you read a lot of books," Bashi was saying.

"He does!" replied one of the entering passengers, who knows me.

"I do read a lot of books."

Everyone else finished boarding, and then he said, "What about guwrible?"

"How do you say it?"

"Guwrible. G, U, L, L, I—"

"Oh, gullible!"

"Gullible." He tried out my pronunciation, stressing the first syllable.

"Yeah, that's like when you believe anything."

"Gullible. It's gotta be G, U."

"Yeah, gullible." I spelled it again. "You know it." I announced the next stop, and as we cruised in I smiled as I heard him continue trying out the word: "Gullible. Gullible."

Nathan Vass

At this point, while stopped at Genessee, another fellow about halfway back began having epileptic fits. He convulsed and screamed in tongues, arching his back toward the high heavens, his legs shooting out, pushing against the seats and walls with Sisyphean force, and continued seizing until the fire department showed up. We sat with all doors open, as people stepped outside, attended to the man on the floor, or looked out the window. Some offered to call for help, which I always appreciate.

"Okay guys, what we're gonna do here is we're gonna wait around for some medical assistance for the gentleman. Thank you for your patience. There should be another number 7 comin' up right behind us pretty soon. If I see him comin' up behind us I'll let you know. Should be just a couple minutes here, love you guys..." and so on. Help arrived in record time, and we were soon free to go. I thanked the passengers profusely for waiting around with me.

Overkill on the positive? Definitely. But fellow operator Neil once wisely noted that on Rainier you can't just kill 'em with kindness; you have to *over*kill them with kindness. Bashi and I got back down to the important stuff.

"It is gullible or gallible?"

"Gullible," I said.

"Should be G, U."

"Yeah, gullible. You know, like the bird, gull, seagull?"

"Gullible. Gull-ible."

"You say it perfect." I'm enjoying this. "Ask me another word!"

"Another word! Exuberant!"

"Exuberant: very, very excited, very happy!"

"Convoluted!"

"Very confused!"

"Man, you got every word! I'm gonna ask you more next time, I'll have more next time!"

"I'm a be ready!"

We know life is a series of highs and lows, but as a bus driver you experience that in a more extreme, much more concentrated fashion. All the highs and lows of life are happening *at the same time*, in a single room, during and inside of each other. I'd been thinking about how to expediently use my break time and remain relaxed on the route. For me it was a pleasant afternoon. For the man convulsing, 8 PM tonight was a disaster. The medics were stressed and concerned, but not as stressed as he was, working what for them was a fairly routine call. Some passengers felt sleepy and used the extra time on the bus to rest; others bit their fingernails or cursed, trying to speed up time. A few enjoyed the chance to step out for a cigarette. And then there was Bashi and me, having our own little spelling quiz and chuckling about it.

Tragedy and comedy rub shoulders in such strange proximity. As the driver, you simply marvel at it all, the level of complexity in all these lives, all happening at once. With enough context it would all make sense, but for the time being, there's nothing to do but marvel.

Which I'm happy to do.

Who was having this intellectually stimulating, cultured, erudite conversation?

COWBOYS OF THE NEW AGE

11/25/2016

"Well, during the time he was alive, *Titus* was his most popular play."

"Really!"

"Yeah, *Titus*, which is interesting because it's so violent. Just outrageous, what they do to one another in that one. And I wonder if that's what drew the crowd back then, you know? But it's a little too much for me, man. In answer to your question, I'd probably say *Macbeth*. 'Cause it has this really, it has this sort of X trajectory between the two protagonists, you know what I'm sayin'?"

"Okay."

"Yeah, 'cause Macbeth starts off being all hesitant to abuse his power and acquire more of it, and Lady Macbeth eggs him on, as you know. But as shit progresses, they begin to switch places, where Macbeth gets more and more power hungry, and Lady Macbeth realizes this shit has gone too far, especially when she gives that sweet monologue towards the end explaining it. So they gradually switch places on the whole corrupting influence of power, which is kinda tight."

"*Coriolanus* is better."

"Really?"

"Yeah."

"I saw the movie version with Ralph Fiennes, but I haven't read it."

"Oh, you gotta read it, bro. But *Hamlet* is Shakespeare's best."

"Oh, totally. It's so huge."

"And Hamlet is only thirty-five! He's a hipster. He's hangin' out with actors and comedians. That's why his dad wants him to kill Claudius. And Romeo, he's nineteen, and Juliet, is, like, twelve."

"Oh God."

Who was having this intellectually stimulating, cultured, erudite conversation? Where were they sitting? What did they look like, and how did they dress?

These were a couple of 'hood brothas riding the bus round about midnight, deep in the bowels of Rainier Valley, Seattle's most crime-infested realm. One was homeless, missing an eye, lugging a backpack and duffel along, the gleaming muscles on his arms sculpted not for show, but from grinding necessity; and the other, tall, wearing oversized gray sweatpants and broad-brimmed skater shoes, the kind you leave untied. His energetic afro practically sprayed out from under his Rainier Beer hat.

You may lie in bed at night, waiting for sleep to beckon. Your mind may drift, wander to the vast nether depths of the city, the blocks of buckled pavement and uncut weeds, the rife low angles of neglect and violence, our very own downtrodden wild west. What are they thinking about, those dark figures in the gloom and rain? What are they saying to each other, right this minute?

Know that sometimes, the cowboys of the new age talk just as they're talking above. Exchanging educated thoughts on life and art, as you and I do, expounding on the great literary works which line my bookshelf, and probably yours too. Thematics and structural organization in Shakespeare plays.

That's the honest truth.

These are the people I most wish to spend time with while I'm at work.

CASCADE OF A THOUSAND COLORS

6/6/2015

I can recall riding the 7 shortly after I'd started at Metro and chatting with the driver. In my later childhood I'd grown up using the route and felt energized as always by its hivelike microcosm of humanity, the earthly globe in all its glorious and terrible wonder compacted into a single vehicle.

"I can't wait to get to drive this," I said to the operator.

"Well, be careful what you say," he murmured. "Give it a try before you say stuff like that." His trepidation was unfounded, as we now know, but he was right to express it. Nobody loves the 7. He had no way of knowing where I was coming from.

The great sea of naysaying bus drivers has subsided over the years. Now people just think I'm crazy. I'm crazier than the passengers I pick up. I get excited when we turn the corner at Pike and a big mob is waiting. I feel humbled and honored to drive alongside so many operators who accept and tolerate my attitude, my enthusiasm that hardly makes sense, but that keeps bubbling out.

Thank you for waving at me, for taking me in despite my gleeful malady of happiness. I don't pretend to understand it, except to say the joy I feel while out here in the vortex is completely real, and utterly soul-satisfying. We yearn to feel whole in this life. And for fleeting moments when directing films, or clicking the shutter, or taking the S-curves at Andover, greeting this new set of eyes and watching them fold into a smile...

A good friend recently rode much of my shift, which was the 7 and the 49 combined (my heart will crumble a little when these routes eventually get split*), and she commented on how much more visibly excited I got once we turned into the 7 and the 7 passengers started getting on. I had never realized a change was visible!

One late night we were at the southbound zone underneath I-90. I was outside the bus, helping a man who was carrying a few upholstered armchairs. We were lifting them on through the back doors of the coach. While we were both back there he gave me his fare, which I took up to the front and paid, bringing him back a transfer.

As I walked up and down the aisle to do this, I had to resist the urge to just sit down next to all the people and ask how they were doing. Dim fluorescents illuminating a cascade of a thousand colors, different moods and tones, lives on their way, the tired and disenfranchised, those who have suffered but hide their bruises, those who recognize kindness and those who don't, a motley marginalized crew of society's unloved, speaking in their native tongues.

These are the people I most wish to spend time with while I'm at work.

---

* The 49 serves the lively (but fast gentrifying) Broadway and U-District corridor in North Seattle; the 7 serves the vast, ethnic, working-class residential tracts of Rainier Valley. Columbia City, in the Valley, is the US's most diverse zip code (98118). The two routes were for three decades one long route (the 7) at all hours; daytime trips were split in 2005 to improve on-time performance. Night trips remain linked for now, saving passengers a transfer.

Nathan Vass

All of which is to say, you youngsters, if your heart is set on something and the old guard tries to dissuade you, consider their opinions, but listen also to yourself. Remember they can only offer their own experience and perspective, which aren't the same as yours. You might be on to something.

We've all
lost, though.

FOR THE SAKE
OF THE OTHERS

5/29/2015

Rachel is a name which has been important in my life. It's also the name of the woman on my bus right now, standing next to me as we float down Rainier Avenue, finishing up the midnight run, drifting ever deeper into the darkest reaches of the Valley.

In a way, the name is fitting, because our conversation somehow turns to matters of great value to me. How did this happen? A second ago we were talking about transferring from the B Line to the 550. Sometimes you know you can go a little further with someone. The air feels right, and before you know it, you're sharing secrets, finessing them toward a more considered polish.

This Rachel was a young soul in an older body, dressed in scruffy black, her sea legs ably keeping balance as we stopped and started. Words flew out of her quickly, a mad and tumbling rush, slurred by both fatigue and enthusiasm—you know that point in the evening, where both seem to hold equal sway?

She'd started things off by thanking me for being a friendly driver, and I'd asked about her commute. Sometimes I couldn't hear her quiet voice as we took the fluttering curves, but I understood when she mentioned she was a widow. I paused, trying to think of how best to share the Alfred Lord Tennyson quote—you know the one—when she just up and said it herself. This is Seattle, where even some of the street folks know Tennyson.

"Well, better to have loved and lost, than to have never loved at all."

"So true. So, so true."

"It's hard though," she said. "To open up. To let yourself love."

"It's *so* hard, once you've lost. It's hard for me to open up, really let go. I'm not good at it." Brandon Street. Can't believe we're talking about this. "I used to be good at it, but once you know how much that type of loss hurts..."

"We've all lost, though."

"That's true."

"You've just gotta do it. We have to allow ourselves to love so that other people can receive it. So they can feel it. People need to feel loved in their lives."

"Oh wow, okay. I'd never thought of it in exactly those terms."

"Yeah. It's not just for us, it's for them. It's like we have a responsibility to be happy. If we're happy, we make the people around us happy. If we're sad, we make everyone around us sad. We *need* to be happy, we need to love. We affect the people around us. It's not selfish. It's our responsibility. You're doing good to the people around you, you know?"

"Yes! Yes!"

"It's like nature, all this green everywhere. Nature's not afraid to grow and change and live. You ever see one tree saying it's better than another tree? Never. Can't be afraid of it."

And just like that, she was out of there.

Nathan Vass

There will always be kind people, and there will always be more kind people than bestial ones.

FECAL AND PHILOSOPHICAL MATTERS

8/18/2013

I pull into Eastlake and Harvard inbound. There's a wheelchair there, a younger vet with one leg. Can't be more than thirty. His remaining leg is in a cast, extending straight out in front of him. Covering him is a T-shirt and soiled blanket. His hair is matted, skin beaten down by the elements; you can't fake long hours spent outside.

He looks up at me with haunted eyes as I pull up and open the doors. "Hi," I say, getting ready to deploy the lift.

"Hey," the man replies in a hoarse voice, immediately continuing: "I have a transfer, but before I even get on I wanna tell you somebody threw a bag a crap at me and so I smell really bad. Can I still ride your bus to Urban Rest Stop and take a shower?"

There are some moments you don't forget. One of them, for me, is the look on this man's face while he waited for me to respond. I couldn't know in that moment he'd asked the same thing of the four previous drivers and been passed up by all of them, meaning he'd been sitting at this stop in his condition for over an hour. I saw only the tired agony of his expression, a face struggling to stay above the surface.

I stepped down toward him. Yes, his clothing and skin were splattered everywhere with fecal matter. No, they didn't smell particularly great. But I've encountered other passengers who've smelled worse; nobody loves the smell of dog feces, but they sure beat human feces in my book. This was rather more on the dog side of things.

"That's all right with me," I said.

After we loaded him up on the lift, I wheeled him back to the wheelchair spot myself, to expedite things and help maneuver his awkward leg cast... but also to let him know he wasn't going to be ostracized or hated during this ride. Sometimes when you do someone a difficult favor, it's tempting to take the opportunity to rub in just how arduous the favor really is; we're not doing that today. I'm not expecting anyone else on this bus to be nice to the guy, but I don't much care what the job-possessing, home-owning commuters think of his being on the bus. This is a public service vehicle. I do my best to make him feel included.

"So tell me again, what happened?"

"Well, I'm out there panhandling, on the side of the street there, when all of a sudden this brand-new Beamer comes driving by and the guy throws a bag of crap at me. And the bag splatters everywhere, and he just drives off."

"Wow. Wow."

"How could someone do that?"

I look back at him. The feces fester in his uncombed hair, his tattered T-shirt, and the wheelchair apparatuses. The lion's share of it is spewed across his wool blanket, which covers his midsection and leg.

I can see now that he's crying.

"I'm already humiliating myself by panhandling, and then he does that on top of that? How could someone do that?" he keeps asking in a sobbing voice. There is no affectation here. "How could there be people that could think like that? It's already hard to lower myself to the level of begging on the street..."

"I can't believe it. I mean, I do believe it, but I just can't believe it. And it wasn't just some old car."

"No, it was a nice BMW."

"Wow. Of course it was. What I'm wondering is, why the heck would anyone be driving around with a bag of crap that big in the first place?"

"No decency. How could he do... and now I smell like this. I'm so sorry, you guys," he says to the people around him. "I'm sorry, miss..."

"Hey, it's not as bad as my dog's farts," says Awesome Tim, from the chat seat.* Awesome Tim is wonderful. At over fifty, he still does heavy outdoor construction work, sunburned down to the last corner of skin, with a tough, Hell's Angels–esque appearance— but a generous heart. He and I talk often. Today, on an unspoken level, he grasps the need to be a sympathetic presence during this man's hard time.

"These women are gonna hate me," the fellow says, as we pull up to Fairview and Yale, where a number of fetching, affluent, well-dressed commuters await.

"Dude," I say, "if one of these people even says a word, I'll back you up a hundred percent. Believe me, man. You got nothin' to worry about."

I don't care if they're all knockouts. Perhaps because of my background and earlier life, there's a nerve in me whose sympathies for the poor and marginalized run impossibly deep. It's almost unreasonable, how much I love these guys. He has no idea how strongly my perspective lies on his side. The women get on without incident.

---

* The name we drivers give to the first passenger seat on the door side, the closest to the driver, for its conversational convenience.

As we approach Urban Rest Stop, the great facility on Ninth between Stewart and Virginia where one can take showers and do laundry for free (and one better—they'll even do your laundry for you), we begin discussing whether we'll get there in time. You can shower until 6 PM—no rush there, it's only 4:50—but we aren't sure if laundry stops at five. Will he be able to wash his clothes? Maybe he could plead his case. Who knows? We got him down there, in any event. He thanked me profusely and headed down the block toward what was probably the best shower of his life.

As I drove away, I couldn't stop thinking about the actions of the BMW driver. Wow, I thought. Just wow. What stunning, embarrassing, appalling hostility. If being human essentially means being empathetic, this sort of sadism exists at the bottom of the spectrum and makes one ashamed to be part of the species. One wishes for sweeping political reform, the kind that would prevent events like this from ever happening again—more accountability for such actions, more resources and upward mobility for the disadvantaged...

However. No amount of politicking or enforcement could ever completely eliminate this type of behavior. There will always be a small percentage of people who enjoy visiting savage and diabolical cruelty on others. And, in like fashion, there will always be a percentage which believes in kindness—and that percentage will always be larger.

What bears this out? Look around us. The best predictor of future behavior is past behavior. In the course of human history, sadism has never been the organizing principle behind human interaction. It wouldn't make sense. In fact, over the centuries, it's been whittled down to almost nothing, to the point that now most of its perpetrators are generally mere individuals, rather than governments, countries, or cultural practices. It is simply in the nature of people to be either kind or neutral, rather than expend energy damaging others. There will always be kind people, and there will always be more kind people than bestial ones.

Nathan Vass

Additionally, there will always be those of us who are disadvantaged. No amount of government programming (Seattle, with its veritable deluge of such, is an example) can eliminate the margins. Laws may eliminate some of the Beamers that drive around with bags of feces, but not all of them (let's hope there was just that one!). Only our kindness can counter such events when they do take place. The generosity we offer can rejuvenate one's belief in the human condition. I speak not of handouts or money, but of something simpler: smiles, eye contact. Acknowledgment. With a gesture, one achieves a purity of immediacy no amount of politicking can duplicate.

And this is good.

All the struggle,
the history, the
prejudice…
like it never
happened,
just for this
one minute.

APPRECIATION

7/10/2013

"Hey," I say.

He's black American, late teens, in spotless oversized black denim and a ski jacket.

"Ey," he responds by default, staring blankly, but then his eyes meet mine, recognizing me, and suddenly he's here. Present. "Hey! How's it goin'?" he says now, getting a little more animated.

"Goin' great, man!" I respond.

"Hey, you think I could get a—"

"Yeah, let's do a trade! None of that 4:30 stuff." That was ages ago. I tear two new transfer tickets. "Fresh off the press right here."

"Fresh off the press," his buddy behind him repeats.

"Oh yeah."

"Word," his friend affirms.

Then the first young man stills himself and says with intention: "Appreciation, dogg."

All the posturing and carefully maintained facades are dropped for a moment as the first guy looks at me with complete candor. We've interacted before, he and I, and his eyes have a light in them whenever I see him; I get the sensation that both of us are excited at the experience of making for ourselves an equal plane, of carving out a judgment-free world, if only for a split moment.

All the struggle, the history, the prejudice... like it never happened, just for this one minute.

"Appreciation," he says again.

"My pleasure."

Nathan Vass

Everyone within earshot—the rich, the poor, the white, and the black—was totally nonplussed for a moment.

"I'M A LIGHT-SKINNED BLACK WOMAN!"

1/18/2013

I heard her before I saw her.

"Don't touch me," the voice said. This is on the 4, going slowly through the Central Area. Loud, belligerent voice, somewhere behind me, escalating, and then finally she stands up, introducing herself to one and all—

"I'M A LIGHT-SKINNED BLACK WOMAN! YOU'RE GON' GET YOUR MOTHERFUCKIN' CRANIUM CRACKED, NIGGER!"

Any driver who's logged enough time on downtown routes knows this woman well. She's one for the ages. The second line she's just blurted out above originates from Dr. Dre's landmark 1992 album *The Chronic*, and as such it's hard for me to take seriously. This gal doesn't look anything like RBX. She doesn't need to, though. With 300 formless pounds, round glasses covering pudgy narrowed eyes, and a stentorian roar of a voice, she leaves an impression.

Her strategy is to lash out at the other customers, in the hope of a response. "Don't touch me," she'll say as boarding passengers brush past her. When they don't sit next to her, she'll blurt out—"You didn't sit next to me because I'm black, huh?!" Woe betide anyone who says anything—anything—in return.

"That dress looks nice," she yelled at a (white) woman sitting across from her one afternoon on the 3.

"Thanks," the commuter said. "That's nice of you to say."

"The red is a nice color."

"I like it."

"It wouldn't work for me though. Wouldn't go well with my COMPLEXION."

Light-Skinned Black Woman—the name she loudly proclaims herself as for all to hear—was clearly hoping for some sort of response. White Commuter Lady did not rise to the bait. A wise move, if I may say so.

The interesting thing about the Light-Skinned Black Woman is not that she hates white people. I'm not surprised by that. What surprises me is that she also hates all black people. And everyone else, too. She's very egalitarian in her hatred. She's awfully generous that way. Doesn't leave anyone out. "I didn't know there were any Jews left in America," she said once, to no one in particular. It's the sort of statement that begs for a contentious reply, and you struggle to refrain from going down that road. It would actually be fine if there were no one else on the bus but her and me; I have the patience to find ways around her bluster.

Other passengers do not.

You can't blame them. The problems generally arise from her pointed comments at others and the resulting back-and-forth escalation. A conversation on a 5 that began with the line "Your dog's cute" ended with her screaming, "I hope your baby fucking dies inside your body, bitch!" at a pregnant woman. Unexpected turns...

Sometimes, if she gets off without things going too badly, I can't help but thank all the other passengers for actively working to make that happen. She's a known quantity in the trenches. We regular bus-riding folk attempt to get along with her, and sometimes it's not so terrible. The folks up front will attempt to keep her distracted long enough to keep her from yelling racial slurs at the top of her lungs. "I couldn't have done that without you guys," I once announced after she'd left. I couldn't keep my tremendous relief to myself.

A story from long ago gets the idea of the LSBW across:

She's at the front of the bus. A tall, built man, in some sort of military uniform, steps on. She engages him immediately with the following: "Hey, Army Guy. I bet they give you a big gun so you can go kill a lotta black people, huh?"

"What?"

"I said, I bet they give you a big-ass gun to go kill niggers with, huh? Government Man, killing black people for money. You probably like it. You like shooting niggers, don't you? Getting medals for it. I bet you kill a whole lotta bl—"

"Lady." The military man is speaking to her firmly and slowly. "Check this out. First of all, this is a *Coast Guard* uniform. And second of all. Maybe you didn't notice it—"(big pause)"—BUT I'M BLACK!"

The bus falls apart laughing. He continues, on a roll—"Girl, you need to start takin' TWO a those pills you take every mornin' instead a just the one, else you best be cuttin' that one pill in HALF, like this..."

After incidents like this and others, I would sometimes think to myself, "There's three million people out here. All of them are welcome on my bus, all of them—except this woman. Everyone else is my buddy. This girl can go jump in the lake."

That type of thought is a problem for me. I don't want to have to fear a certain passenger. I want to, within reason, be able to let anyone on the bus. Once she made my happy 4 devolve into one very unhappy 4, and afterward I felt relieved in the sense that, well, at least I won't see her for a while. Somehow you don't see her except occasio—

No. I was wrong. There she was the very next day, big and bright as life, right there at Third and Union. Noises build to a crescendo in the Central District, as we approach 23rd Avenue.

LSBW: Don't touch me," she says to the two (black American) teen-age girls sitting right behind me. "You guys are probably lesbians.

Girl 1:   The fu—what this girl jus' say to me?

Girl 2:   I think she done said—

LSBW: I said don't touch me, faggot!

Girl 1:   Lady, what the hell you talkin' 'bout?

LSBW: Keep your hands to yourself.

Girl 2:   This girl need to shut the fuck up—

Girl 1:   Hold up. I didn't say nothin' to you. Ain't nobody bothering your big ass, why you tryna start some shit?

LSBW: Stop trying to touch me with your hands that you've been masturbating with!

Girl 2:   Wha—

Girl 1:   The fuck is this bullshit? I didn't say—

LSBW: You been touchin' yourself with those hands, I don't want germs comin' from your hands gettin' on me.

Girl 2:   Hold up. This bitch say we les?

Girl 1:   The fuck is you talkin' 'bout? Tryna say some shit about me that isn't true, callin' me lesbian, the fuck is your problem... dirty hands? What the fuck? I don't wanna touch your ugly ass. Stay the hell away from me.

Girl 2:   Yeah, tha's right. You don't wanna touch me, don't fuckin' touch me, girl—

LSBW: Don't pretend you ain't no lesbian, bitch. YOU BEEN MAS-TURBATING WITH THOSE HANDS! Don't touch me!

Girl 1:   Ah can't believe this girl. I didn't say a motherfuckin' thing to you, I's just mindin' my own business and now you be assaulting me, attackin' my character tha's what this is—

Girl 2:   Man, your hands is probably dirtier than anybody's. Look at 'em—

Nathan Vass

LSBW: Stop bothering me!

Girl 1:   Okay, now that shit is funny. It's you that gots to stop both-
          erin' me.

Girl 2:   Go sit somewhere else, you don't like us.

Girl 1:   Go sit in the back. Stop bothering me.

LSBW: You guys need to go get abortions—

Girl 1 is nonplussed. The situation is so absurd she's more surprised
than angry. Foul-mouthed as she may sound, she has not called
LSBW any derogatory name. You can tell her profane self comes
from a good place, and that she just wishes to cap the situation.
She's trying to apply reason to what's going on. It's not working.
In her astonishment she attempts a quick recap of the proceedings
before launching further—

Girl 1:   What. The. Fuck is you talkin' about, sister? Man, you is
          an embarrassment to the people, takin' a shit like that up
          in here. Firs', you be sayin' to everybody on this bus that
          me an' my friend is lesbians. Then, you be stirrin' some
          ca-razy mothafuckin' bullshit about I don't even know what
          the fuck—

Me: (Stopped and turning around) Hey. Whoa. Hey, HEY. Hey!
          Both a you are WAY better than this. Ain't nobody need to
          be yellin' about lesbians and abortions. We can talk about
          that later. I need both of you to do me a special favor. Don't
          say nothin'. I know she's bothering you, I know both of you
          wanna say some stuff, but please. I'm askin' you for ten
          minutes.

Girl 1:   I'm a get the fuck off this bus, is what I'm gon' do. Come
          on, Keesh, les' go. You have a good day, bus driver. Sorry
          we got into such a big argument.

Me: Oh man, you know it ain't your fault. You guys have a good
          rest of the day. I'm sorry this happened!

Girl 1:   Me too! You have a good night too!

Afterward, LSBW and I struck up a conversation. A friend of mine attends the same church she goes to, where she apparently behaves herself; she has to be civil sometime. She was on her way to her mother's house, and she told me about the fried chicken she was going to eat. It was a relief to get her to talk to me instead of bothering other people—let alone have a nonracist conversation at that. Could I be so lucky? She loves talking about the (stunningly unhealthy) food she enjoys.

I was writing above about the worrying thought that I might have to refuse her service. I'm troubled by the idea of rejecting someone because of who they are, as opposed to their particular behavior on a specific day. The latter makes sense. The former rubs against my conception of how I would like to treat people. There was a time (after she told the pregnant woman to have a miscarriage) where I wasn't quite sure where I stood on that line. I mused over the implications one day while driving the 5, back in the days when it turned into the 54/55 to West Seattle. You have a lot of time to think when driving. I pulled into the zone at Third and Pike, now an outbound 55. A lot of activity here, milling about, people getting on and off—

"EXCUSE ME DO YOU GO TO 35TH AND AVALON?"

There she is, big as life once again. You could've heard her yell the question from a block away. The awful truth is, well, I do go to 35th and Avalon. I hesitate for a split second before timidly saying, "Yeah, I do."

"Good!" she yelled. "I need to go to 35th and Avalon. I need to get there before 6."

"Oh, we'll get there before 6. We'll probably get there at 5:30." It's barely 5. She's got one thing over on a lot of other passengers—she can plan in advance!

Now, I'm petrified. The 55 is an entirely Caucasian crowd. It's the height of PM rush hour, and everyone on the bus is white, and each one of them is wearing a suit. We're about to get on the viaduct, where it would be very awkward to pull over if something happens.

And something is simply *bound* to happen with this volatile mixture—a standing load of 80 white commuters who've been working all day, and one very unhappy Light-Skinned Black Woman.

She goes and sits down somewhere right behind me, where I can't see her through my mirror. I expect the heavens to fall. I'm bracing myself... and then, it's the funniest thing.

Nothing happens. There is silence.

She doesn't say anything to anyone, and nobody says anything to her. At the end of the ride I took a big, huge leap of faith, going out on what felt like a very precarious limb—I almost squeaked out the words, pretty sure they were a big mistake—

"Have a good day..."

But no! She responded with the world's gruffest version of "Thank you! God bless you!"

Afterward I thought, Wow. She took the right dosage of meds today, that's for sure. How fantastic. After that day I always give her the benefit of the doubt, like I do with everyone else. Because sometimes she doesn't make anyone cry. Once, in a moment that should've caused an earthquake because of its shattering unexpectedness, she bumped into someone's dog—and *apologized!*

She's definitely still the Light-Skinned Black Woman, however. Make no mistake. As she got off at Virginia one afternoon, after I went out on a limb yet again and told her to "have a good one," she responded with something more along the lines of what I'd expected the first time—

"STOP FLIRTING WITH ME BECAUSE I'M BLACK!"

That's more like it. Everyone within earshot—the rich, the poor, the white, and the black—was totally nonplussed for a moment. As soon as she was gone, we all started laughing.

To be here
is to know
the human
organism,
unadorned.

ODE TO AURORA

2/12/2013

I've sided with my friends in the past when we deplored the visual aesthetic of Aurora. Was there an uglier strip of road in the city? This is what we asked ourselves, tearing down the six-lane expanse at okay, something rather above the speed limit, peering out from our cars in derision.

That was then. We were youngsters, and we thought we knew what we were talking about. We didn't. There are things—worlds, lives, and loves—that you'll never know if you only ever drive through a place. Get out of the car. Feel that wind blowing your hair. Know the feeling of walking in the cold, on this day, these sidewalks. Birds, noise, exhaust, voices.

Let some dirt get under your fingernails.

I have come to love the iconography of Aurora Avenue. Here is a realm that stands outside of time. There is the egregious concrete expanse, nigh uncrossable, a rotating pulse of endless, ongoing life, rubber tires uniting to make a sound we can't reduce to a name.

It's the sound of a thousand stories, elated, pathetic, tragic, energized. Normal. There are the decaying sidewalks and the stretches without them, cement plates buckling under the onset of nature.

There's the veritable battery of motels and hotels, room after sordid room, and who's counting. Years of secrets lining the fading walls; how many times have these drapes opened and closed? Standing in an empty bedroom, staring nowhere. Sometimes you can hear an echo in the hum of a fluorescent lamp.

The landscape of Aurora Avenue holds firm against the leveling advances of technology. This could be the eighties. Tire rotation, junk removal, appliance demolition, the dollar stores; block after block of chain-link fences and used car lots. The Elephant at 8800. Aurora Donuts. Dang's Hair Salon. St. Vincent de Paul—once a word for a man, now immortalized into another kind of life. These are the edifices of our time. Lowes. *The Korea Times.* Dilapidated tattoo parlors and auto wrecking lots that seem deserted. Men slink around in the darkened corners.

The receding concrete vastness rolls away endlessly, populated at all hours of the day. Detox and rehab facilities pepper the landscape. I remember a prostitute at 115th, turning down a free bus ride even though there was snow on the ground, choosing to look for work at 5 AM; another now sorts through her plastic bag of condoms. Her mother is sitting next to her.

Craggy eyes and broken faces peering at me in the dark. A man gets on with a full-size camping tent, big enough for four people, like it wasn't any big deal: just goin' up the street. Another fellow, a middle-aged white homeless man, his face utterly destroyed, beaten to a pulp. The skin has turned black, and the cuts on the eyebrows are drying. He's lost his backpack with his HIV paperwork and his last $100. Tough-looking character, but his voice is human. I can't tell if he's crying.

I do my best, staying with him, staying present. Another man and his friend thank me because I let him ride yesterday, though he was 60 cents short. Here's the methadone crowd, wide awake already, as I advertise the clinic at 165th and 170th—"These next

Nathan Vass

two stops both pretty good for THS," I tell them on the mic. "Good day today. Maybe see you on the way back!"

The reaches quiver with life out here. You *have* to talk to people. Connections mean something, however faint; the street denizens engage each other even if they're initially strangers. Sometimes they tear each other apart; other times they bond in ways they never knew—"Small world," you hear someone say, with that familiar tone of welcome incredulity. What commuters there are often keep to themselves, perhaps out of fear, or perhaps knowing that this just isn't their element.

I help a couple with their six suitcases and duffel bags. "I should work at an airport," I quip, as they toss bags to me, which I heave onto the sidewalk. Laurie's sitting across the aisle, explaining about vomiting and Pepsi. Her day's better now than it was earlier. Sometimes her blood pressure's too low.

"It says I'm dead, is what it says," she intones with listless eyes.

"I don't believe that for a second," I smile back.

Here's a man with his own swivel chair, unidentifiable wooden cartons, and dog. Gent with a jacket that may have been yellow in another life, the putrid stench of urine clinging to him and his five bags. He's tall and quiet; think Clint Eastwood if *Rawhide* had never panned out.

Often the thought comes up, again—I wouldn't want to be spending time with any other group of people right now.

How can I want to be here, not as some mere passing anthropological diversion, but day after day after day? What is this feeling that grows richer with the passing of time? What could I possibly be so enamored with? Aurora Avenue? What?

To be here is to know the human organism, unadorned.

I want to feel the truth of life, the tactile earth of the ordinary. These are not extreme lives, but people like me. A veneer that's present elsewhere has been stripped away, and my head feels clear down on the ground. Diversity paradoxically reminds us of how similar we all are. Commonalities show themselves. There is a confirmation of sorts taking place—yes, we are human. I find this deeply comforting. This is all on top of the fact that I can help someone, or perhaps alter the state of people's minds, even for a moment—something about that allows all this to work together, the acts of observing and participating mingling into something new.

We can forget the savagely indifferent balance of nature. Out here you are confronted with it. Classrooms teach children that there is an answer to every question. Only on the outside do we discover how little quantifiable facts count for in life. A line is brought to mind, from Andrei Tarkovsky's *Solaris*: "In man's endless search for truth, he finds only knowledge."

To be slapped in the face with reality, to live in realms of truth regardless of positive and negative—this is an affirmation of life that I benefit from. Despite all the things you might know or have seen, you can still look out at the world with a sense of wonder. There is something about physical reality that is inherently satisfying to me. It always has a new shade to reveal, if you're open to it.

A spry, tough, older guy with a white ponytail, John, told me one night—"You are *The Beast*, man. You're changing what Aurora Avenue is, just by being out here. Dude. I've watched you. Everything you say and act to these people... you are THE BEAST!"

To which I replied, "No, you're the beast, man—"

"No no no, I'm not the friggin' beast, dude. That doesn't make any sense. YOU'RE the Beast. Don't be modest, man..."

I smiled.

Is she a stronger person now, though, than she was before?

INDIA

7/31/2014

I see her brighten the bus stop as I pull up. Third and Union south-bound, sometime before midnight. Hers is a smile which renders her ageless; you see the girl she used to be, echoes of a happier time. She's thirty-five and thin, ready to go home now, rich black hair tied in a workaday ponytail, unbrushed for now.

I've seen her before. Why does she smile so when she sees it's me driving? Perhaps she feels safer on my 7, or maybe she just enjoys the warm vibes. I greet everyone with enthusiasm. I get excited when we're full up and late on the 7 at night. There are times when I feel myself bubbling over, thrilled beyond measure to be here, can't hide it, thrilled to be in the vortex, Metro's busiest route,* the throbbing heart of this great city, maybe even—dare I say it? Changing the atmosphere just by being myself, reaching out to all these lives as though they were my friends—because of course, they are. This euphoric bliss happens delicately, seemingly without my trying, and I feel lucky to touch it when it's here.

Tonight I gab with various folks. Just passing the time. Here's a Jack-in-the-Box employee and I, discussing the value of being a people person at our respective jobs. Tonight he's looking for a pay phone, and we wonder where any are. Another man extols the virtues of his bicycle's disc brakes after I ask. Disc brakes on a bike seem luxurious to me. They're great going down McClellan Hill, apparently.

Eventually she steps up to the front. At first I think she's getting off at an earlier stop tonight, but no, she just wants to talk. She's happy to try, despite the trouble of speaking the new language. I feel honored that she feels comfortable enough to do so. Would you do the same in her place? It's no easy feat, making small talk in a language and country that aren't your own, but sometimes the feeling of connection is worth it.

"Are you just getting off work?" Yes, she is. An Indian accent. "You work late," I marvel, noting the clock: 11:41. "Do you like it?"

She waxes and wanes in response, smiling, agreeing with my hand gesture of "more or less."

"A job is a job," she says finally.

"It's true, a job is a job. A good thing to have."

She explains that back home, people did laundry for her. Servants took care of stuff like that. Now, not only does she do her own laundry, she does everyone else's, for work. A completely different world. She cried at first, disillusioned, feeling lied to by the Great Dream, disappointed and alone on a crushingly fundamental level. She and her sister moved halfway around the globe and here she is now, mopping floors, working part-time here and there, long and

---

* When combined with the 49 ridership. Night trips remain linked for now, saving passengers a transfer. The route path of the two lines, from the U-District to Capitol Hill to Downtown to Rainier Valley, remains the core travel pattern for Seattle, as evidenced by Sound Transit's inaugural light rail line effectively shadowing the 7/49.

Nathan Vass

late hours, menial labor seven thousand miles from home. Fixing the dry-cleaning machine, struggling to keep her tears to herself.

She's been in the States three years and has lived that entire time on Rainier Avenue. What a notion of America she must have, so specific to her experience. How little those around her know of her past. Take a second look at the gas-station attendants, the gardeners and cooks around you. Some of them used to be dignitaries, scientists, and more before they came over. A good friend of mine was once assistant vice president at the University of Tehran. Now he drives a bus. His passengers get on without a clue.

Ernst Gombrich once wrote that an accent is a badge of honor. It means that person, or their family, possessed the unthinkable courage to completely restart their lives from scratch, with no safety net, in a place they don't know and often are not welcome in. That, we can agree, is fortitude.

Is she a stronger person now, though, than she was before, moving beyond all those years of soft living? I think so. The expanded perspective, the seeds for empathy, the learned skill of appreciation... Out loud I say, "Well, it makes your character stronger. You know?"

She gets it. "Yes, it's true."

"And you are always so happy, smiling. Every time." She beams anew in the darkness. "As long as you can be happy, people can be happy, that is very impressive to me. Anyone really, who can be happy in this life."

She affirms the sentiment, and I continue, "I *love* driving the bus! Helping all the people, talking to people..."

Now she's laughing, in surprise, delight, in newfound freedom. You can make the most out of anything.

"Where you are from?" she asks. It's normally a question I don't care for, but I know what she means.

"Korean."

She's happy at the response, excited at the commonality of displacement. She asks for a night stop, thirty feet closer to her apartment, and thirty feet away from the drugged-out thugged-out ghettotastic reunion that's forever taking place in the bus shelter, over there by the gas station, the omnipresent hustle that always looks more dangerous than it is, bubbling on just this side of violence. Those thirty feet make all the difference. Thanking me, she dashes off into the shadows. She has her keys ready.

They crash through life, but they stick around each other, for better or worse.

FIGHTERS AND LOVERS, IN AND OUT OF TIME

3/2/2017

Small talk up front, like any other night. At Eighth and Jackson I said, "Yeah, I'm gonna roll this 'til one o'clock or so. I think I'm a little less than halfway through." I grabbed the mic to tell them. "All right this is a number 7 tonight, goin' to Rainier Beach—"

"Whoooo!" An appreciative holler from the back.

"Oh yeah! Number 7 right here, this particular bus only goes as far as Henderson…"

Did I call the fight into being by naming the route? Is that how it works? The movement was as scrambled as the noise, and sudden. It was dim, tinted glass windows reflecting the swelling melee inside, cool fluorescents glistening off jackets and limbs as they stuttered forward, like a camera on slow shutter. Dark shades of fabric against green seats.

I was not afraid. In my experience, when you are unfailingly kind to each passenger, the energy of a fight will only ever involve other people, not you. Plus, the rest of the bus will be on your side. Nothing is more powerful than how you treat others.

I didn't even have to say anything. A bystanding passenger yells: "Hey, no fightin' on the bus! No fightin' on the bus, quit startin' that!"

Another customer calls out, "Hold on hold on hold on." These are two African-American gents attempting to redress the situation, one of whom I'd been chatting with a moment ago. What's going on? A young Caucasian man with an unsettling face, something unhinged here, speaking in low tones to John, a curly haired Latino and regular rider. I notice Valerie, John's wife (also Latina), seated nearby. John's angry, hoarse as he expresses his thoughts to the creepy quiet fellow.

I can't remember if I was on the mic or just shouting. "All right, we gotta stay friendly. We gotta keep it friendly. Gentlemen, my man, let's sit down, keep it simple."

Bystanding Redresser A calls out again, "No fightin' on the bus!"

When people are fighting, you have to say things several times to arrive at the effect one normally achieves when saying something just once. They're distracted, after all.

I'm on the microphone now. Speak loudly, clearly. "I'm gonna pull over right here, guys keep it cool, we're gonna stay friendly."

Bystanding Redresser B echoes my sentiments, but more bluntly: "Go siddown!"

John's standing on the seats, shouting. He's closer to me. Creepy Guy is slinking toward the back, unwilling to get punched but willing to make verbal jabs.

I try to contribute something amiable to all this. "Nothin's wrong, everything's right, we're gonna keep it low key tonight, keep it light—"

John to Creepy Guy: "You started it!"

Valerie: "John! John!"

Redresser B: "Check it, dogg, for real—"

Valerie: "You wanna go to jail don't wanna go to jail? Don't wanna go to jail over this."

Forget the mic. I'm yelling over all of them. He's a friend of mine, I'm thinking. What's he doing? "STAY COOL JOHN, STAY COOL, IT AIN'T NOTHIN'."

"But she started—"

"CALM DOWN, THANK YOU. It's all good, it's all good." New passengers are still coming into the bus. Can you believe it? In one breath I say to the newcomers, "Hey, how ya doin'?" followed by a bark at the interior: "STAY COOL, GENTLEMEN."

Creepy Guy, baiting from the rear: "Fuck you want? Fuck is that—"

John cries, "WHATEVER." Hear the energy on the downbeat of his "WHA—." A caged animal, righteous anger ready to fight.

Redresser A: "Get that man off. He need to go."

The dynamic is interesting. All but one of the principals are over forty and momentarily putting aside their racial differences. Redresser A, B, and Valerie are united in trying to calm down John. Those four are of a piece in the way Creepy Guy, a pale and pimply twenty-something, isn't. He's still back there, palming his PBR, staring balefully. Alcohol brings out the worst in people.

I'm saying, "We're just gonna let it go, it's okay. It's okay."

A voice says, "She started it."

John steps off the seat and into the aisle, starts to calm down. "Sorry 'bout that, Nate."

"It's okay John, no worries no worries. Just gonna forget about it. Be the bigger man." He sits. Creepy Guy has exited the open back door, which I immediately close before he can reenter. We're on the old bus tonight, thank goodness—the doors on the new buses are programmed so they can't close that quickly. A "safety" feature.

John winds out, a long breath escaping. I say to him and everyone else, "Thank you! 'Preciate it, guys."

And just like that, Redresser A asks me: "Ey, you ever had wasabi?"

Talk about letting bygones be bygones! I do my best to follow his lead without losing a beat. "Wasabi tastes goooood!"

"Ha!"

"It's strong though, I can't have too much of it. Clear out your nose in a second!"

"I know das right. Nothin' like it."

Someone else joins in, and they have their wasabi conversation. Who made it, is it a root, what are the principal ingredients. I look up in the mirror at John and Valerie.

I felt something similar, looking at them now, to what I felt when I first saw Michelangelo's *Pietà* in Rome. I stumbled upon it by accident in my travels there. I wanted to see it but imagined it wouldn't fit on my already dense list of things to take in. It's on the right side of the main entrance to St. Peter's Basilica. I happened to glance over and recognized it instantly. I smiled the gentle smile of a surprise felt in solitude, and I stood there a long while, the better to let the emotions of the piece reach me. I'm one of those people who stands forever in front of art pieces.

For me, the *Pietà* is a portrait of a mother's love and sorrow for her adult son. Michelangelo's statue specifically renders Mary as more youthful than most *Pietàs*, and this emphasizes the love being depicted as a woman's love for a man, platonic, familial, everlasting.

Valerie cradled John's head as Mary does in Michelangelo's vision. In both cases, I saw love suffusing great strife: two humans in each other's arms now, two wayward souls I've seen for years, the perennial couple of Rainier Avenue, getting back together as often as they break up. They crash through life, but they stick around each other, for better or worse. Something keeps them in each other's good graces, and they are by now a single entity more than two separate individuals, and my favorite moments of theirs are when I see the tenderness I see now.

He deflated, returning to his better self. She held him tightly and delicately at the same time, running fingers through his curly locks. Passing underneath the freeway, orange sodium lights wafting in on their life-battered faces. Was the love between them, which kept their better angels afloat, any less true, any less real than that between a homeless man and his grieving mother, two thousand years ago?

"Oh baby," she whispered. "Can't do like tonight." Quiet voices, working toward a common ground.

"That guy was talkin' to you wrong."

"I know."

"Nobody talks my wife like that."

"I know, but it's just words, honey."

"My wife though, talkin' 'bout my wife, you,"

"It ain't nothin' to me. You got to promise me. He ain't right in the head, you know. Gotta keep your head right. I don't care if they bitch at me. Man, bus driver, he's no disrespectin' man."

"Oh, it's all good," I said.

"My husband," she said.

"He's a good guy," I replied.

She looked out the window, his head still in her arms. Finally she spoke, mostly to herself.

"I'll love him 'til my heart give out."

Did we always make the decisions we make now?

RESPECT, CURRENCY OF THE STREET

5/18/2016

He was a strapping young man in his forties, built, the kind you don't want to mess with. Those construction boots looked steel-toed, and his muscles gave heft and shape to his weathered letterman. Evenly spaced cornrows stretched his dark scalp tight. Although he wasn't giving me the dead eyes, you know he had the look down, practiced to a withering tee. I asked him how he was doing. He reached into a back pocket.

"Hol' up. I got it somewhere. I'm a find it right quick."

"It's all cool."

"Naw, I got it."

He was sitting behind me now, across from another man I recognized as one of the regular fixtures at the Rainier/MLK interchange. That man, a dealer clad in a dilapidated down jacket and black beanie, watched our friend across the aisle.

"Man, where I put that thing," the first fellow muttered, searching for his fare. "I had it. Ah *know* I had it."

"He don't care, dude."

"Naw, man."

"This bus driver don't care," said Mr. Beanie, trying to de-stress his neighbor.

"Naw, man. It ain't *about* that. I bet he hear a thousand excuses a day. I want him to know I'm for real."

The other man responded with chagrined silence. Most of us are in a position to both survive and be principled, simultaneously. But...

We wander about in our lives, and our priorities lean and grow, circumstances and decisions exerting a subtle pressure. Did we always make the decisions we make now? Have we compromised ourselves somewhere along this gradual journey? The day-to-day has a way of hiding things. Have we exchanged integrity for convenience unbeknownst to ourselves, or will the child within still recognize itself in the mirror?

Whatever the first man, Mr. Cornrows, has going on in his life, principles still figure largely in his value system, and I imagine he's all the better for it.

You can
always
hang out
on my bus...

IT'S NEVER OVER 'TIL IT'S OVER

8/13/2017

She looked apprehensive.

I probably did too. The clock had just struck midnight, and angry voices boomed in our periphery. She was out there, waiting for the bus in a white and yellow summer dress, breezy, perhaps wishing there was someone around, anybody, besides this angry yelling man approaching. I was inside my darkened bus, waking up disoriented from a short nap. The shift was almost done, and it had been a breeze... but it's never over 'til it's over.

Bus drivers sometimes ride my bus to get a feel for the night 7, different ways of handling it. Certain passenger friends call a ride on my 7 "Bus Therapy," while some drivers have dubbed it "The Nathan Vass Refresher Course." I doubt it qualifies for that lofty moniker (I prefer calling it my "office hours"), but I did have an evening where three operators, unbeknownst to each other, all came out to ride the last half of my shift. I was telling them it's never over until it's completely over, 'til you've parked the bus on the lane inside the yard. You could be a hundred feet away from home base, and it could all still fall apart.

As it happened, we *were* about a hundred feet away from home base, these drivers and I, wrapping up the shift, when... wouldn't you know it, a woman came running out of the bushes with blood on her hands and waist, waving her arms and asking us for assistance with her boyfriend, who had been stabbing her.

It's never over 'til it's over.

We called for help and she got the assistance she needed. I try not to offer relationship advice to random strangers, but given the circumstances...

"Um. You might think about dumping this guy," I said.

"Oh God yes," she said.

It was with these thoughts that I stood and stretched out of my nap. Some real angry voices out there. I sighed. It didn't matter how carefree the day had been. In its last minutes you still might have to step up, summon your better angels, and steer the moment as best you can.

I opened the door and turned on the interior lights. Summer Dress and I made nervous eye contact, neither one of us quite sure what was transpiring. She was still standing out there, I was standing by the farebox, as a belligerent voice came closer...

"Hi," I said to her with kind eyes. Any friendly stranger is a friend, not a stranger, in an intense situation.

"Hey," she replied. Cute blue eyes, short, with headphones she knew not to be listening to right now.

"DON'T NOBODY TALK TO ME THAT WAY," said a tall man in dark clothes and a beanie, a bass-inflected gravel rasp to his throaty din. It sounded vaguely familiar: where've I heard that voice before? Ah, yes. I put it together right before I saw his face. Marcus loomed out of the shadows, walking down from the bus behind me.

Boy, does it ever pay off to know a man's name.

You never know when you'll see someone again, or how. The genial history he and I have paid off in spades now. The present instantly defused, and the girl's eyes lit up with surprise, comfort, and relaxation as I said in a friendly tone just a tad quieter than normal:

"Hey, Marcus." Pause. "You don't sound too happy."

He exhaled. Calming down. "Naw, man. This guy trying to tell me to 'take my shit and get off the bus.'"

"You can always hang out on my bus..."

"Ah know. But this guy's just..."

"I'm sorry to hear it, dude. You know you can always hang in here."

The young lady was searching her purse for change. She looked up at him, saying, "Oh, you go ahead."

I think Marcus realized then that he was scaring people. He looked at her now, over the rims of his wire-frame glasses, not lasciviously but how a father looks at girls his daughter's age: with caring. I love watching people think. He deflated further back to his normal self and said, "Oh, no. I *always* let ladies go first."

He smiled and she returned the same, feeling the tension slack loose.

I said, "So he was givin' you some attitude?"

Marcus didn't even need to vent. "I'm okay," he said wearily. "It's just too hot for all that!"

"Yeah, we gotta keep it low-key!"

Tone of voice. Choice of words. I've asked hundreds of people, including Marcus himself, to step off the bus at various ends of the line. I've never *told* them to though, and I've definitely never used the words he quoted the other (brand new) driver as saying. If I told all those people to "take their shit and get off my bus," I don't think I would even be *alive*. Instead I have the respect of friends in more corners of society than I ever could have imagined, corners I never knew existed. Seeing the young woman realize she could relax, that everything was okay, that for some reason this driver knew this guy by name and they could talk things down... I didn't know that would be the highlight of my night.

It's never over 'til it's over.

She laughed the laugh of new wisdom, of the relief that comes with seeing things in a new light, an easier light.

THE LINES THAT MAKE US

10/11/2017

"Aaaahh," she shrieked. She was referring to her bag of groceries.

Getting on the bus had been difficult, a challenge involving balance and a careful hold for an aging body. Nothing in life prepares us for the challenge of decrepitude, the humility of being reduced to a child, guided down a hallway by hospital staff, taking our first steps after weeks in bed with a walker and their help.

We used to be so good at this.

I gave her the time she needed to settle in, but not quite enough—I started rolling out slowly with one of my customary "hang on tight" announcements before she had completely sat down. The groceries slipped—they were falling, until they weren't. She caught them in time.

"You okay?"

"Yeah," she said. "My grocery bags almost flew everywhere, but I got 'em."

"Well, even if it just barely works out, it still works out, right?"

There's something about certain cast-off sentences I've heard people say, the way they hang in the air. In a moment of conversation they'll drop a nugget of wisdom without thinking. They're just being themselves. It's no big deal for them. But for me, meanwhile, their throwaway line will have enormous resonance. I'll sit with it, keep it in my mental pocketbook of how to think, how to live. Such lines have proved formative for me.

I could see by this elderly woman's reply that I had had that effect on her. She laughed the laugh of new wisdom, of the relief that comes with seeing things in a new light, an easier light, the place where things make sense. It's not so bad after all.

Hanging on by a thread still qualifies, absolutely and irrevocably, as hanging on.

Nathan Vass

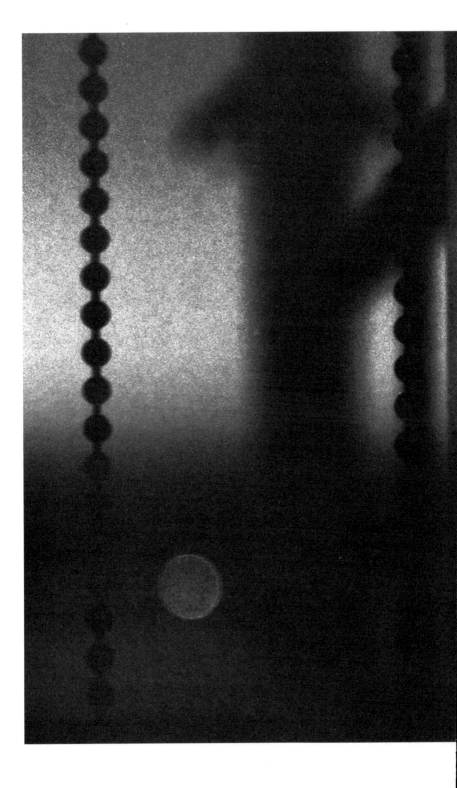

I want him to feel welcome.

THOUGHT I HEARD SOMETHING

11/5/2013

We're getting on into the evening. My last passenger of the night is an older African-American gentleman. Often he can be seen sitting on the sidewalk outside Bartell's at Third and Union. He was there earlier and is now getting on at Pine southbound; I imagine he didn't find quite what he was looking for at the open-air marketplace that is Third and Pine. It's time for him to check out the other drug bazaar, Third and James.

Arthur Conan Doyle once noted that worlds of considerable complexity and size can coexist in the same physical space with relative invisibility to each other; different levels of life swirl around us as we, unbeknownst, drift through. These layered milieus often take form in the eyes of others only through instances of unexpected violence, which is unfortunate.

While in some cities different standards of behavior are more markedly relegated by geography, Seattle is a touch more enthusiastic in fulfilling the American notion of the melting pot. Here it is possible to walk through the southeast corner of Third and Pine in fancy heels, with shopping bags in hand—without knocking the balance of worlds out of order. That this doesn't happen a hundred percent of the time is one of the great urban tragedies. Though, having said that, just yesterday I watched a collage of dealers and shakers at the aforementioned corner. They parted like the Red Sea for two European seniors, who passed through none the wiser. *That* doesn't happen in every city. The connection point for all these worlds is our shared humanity.

To return to our friend, now headed for James Street. Most homeless people in the US are white males between thirty and fifty, with quite a few reaching into their sixties;* aside from his race, this fellow fits the upper end of the bill, with his bald pate and sad eyes, red Adidas sweatpants today, gracing a hollow frame with no context.

What is his story? Who once held this being in her loving mother's arms, and who used to value this man's company, his wit and soul? Did he dream of the great things he could one day accomplish, and still can?

I won't find out tonight, because his toothless gums are vibrating against each other. His is a withdrawal so extreme he cannot speak and can hardly control his muscles; they spasm quietly as we pass under the orange lights. Before, during, and after I greet him, his song is a funereal dirge of helpless groans, a repeating grunt I know from moments of extreme pain. He sits up front staring nowhere, unresponsive and moaning as I ask after his welfare and mention the weather, filling out the spaces with pleasant noise. I want him to feel welcome.

"Here we are now, looks like Third and James, made it here in one piece,"

"Uuuuh, uuuuh."

---

* Source: The 2011 Annual Homeless Assessment Report to Congress (published 2012), the be-all end-all for homeless statistics.

Nathan Vass

"Lemme get close to the curb for ya." Pause. "Did you want this one?"

"Uuuh."

"Are you gonna be able to stand up okay? Can I help you stand?"

"Uu-uuu, uh."

The faintest glimmer of recognition in his eyes, for a fleeting moment—that's him in there, that's you, that's me!

"Lemme help out. Make it a little easier. I'm just gonna reach under your shoulder here, and then we'll stand up together. Sound cool?"

I power him up gently. "There you go my friend, there it is... okay. You take care tonight, be careful now. And oh, don't forget your cup of coins there, don't wanna leave that behind."

"Uuuuh."

"I'll see you again."

All the while: "Uuuh, uuuuh, uuh," disappearing into the shadowy recesses. Figures meld with each other in the low light.

A dear friend of mine has a six-year–old daughter, whom I consider a friend in her own right. One evening we were walking out to her car, and I was carrying little Athena, by now fast asleep. Into her dreaming ears I whispered, "You're one of my good friends, Athena. I love you very much."

Nobody heard me. She definitely didn't. She was shifting in my arms in slumberland, busy making new memories. But there's a part of you that believes in some sort of osmosis, in the magic of things unknown, of stars and souls and moving time. I was yielding to this romantic notion, believing in her sleepy murmur, or the glimmer in the man's eyes. I doubt either of these two understood my words to them in the moment, but that's okay. I say the lines to be myself, and to share, if not the literal meaning, the tone.

Sometimes all that matters is the tone, a distant kindness from far away.

Speak loudly, confidently, kindly—thank you for waiting, thanks for your patience, I appreciate your patience tonight.

BLACK LIVES

8/15/2016

It all started somewhere northbound on Tenth Avenue East, as we drifted past Saint Mark's Cathedral. There's never any traffic here, but there was tonight. Whirling lights flashing up ahead, passersby on the sidewalk with cradled arms, hands on hips. We, in the bus, had just driven all the way up from Rainier Valley and were in the home stretch, through residential north Capitol Hill on our way to the U-District terminal.

This is normally the easy part.

Police cruisers in the distance inched forward. What with the long line of cars and *three* other 49s in front of me, I couldn't make out what was happening. It took forever for me to realize it was a protest. Of course. But what were they doing out here in the 'burbs? People protest on Broadway, or downtown, not Tenth Avenue. There's nothing out here but houses, and all the lights were turned out. These poor protesters were their own audience.

Eventually, after *six* of us 49s—a staggering hour and a half's worth of bus service stacked up in the same place—got locked in a standstill amongst an endless line of cars, the protesters' plan began to emerge. By now we had spilled out of our parked vehicles and were standing in the street chatting. We were in the quiet realm, a good half-mile away from the action, living in the charged calm that lies on the peripheries of an event. Passengers fell asleep or else abandoned ship, choosing to walk. We began learning this was a Black Lives Matter protest on its way to the mayor's home—hence the reason for masses of people blocking roadways in unconcerned sleepy residential neighborhoods.

I've written before on the disconnect between protesters and the groups of people those protesters are supporting. The dichotomy is never more apparent than during Black Lives Matter protests. To explain:

For the lion's share of this protest's routing, it blocked and completely destroyed service on only one bus route—*the single most essential conduit to the black neighborhoods in South Seattle*—the 7/49.

The irony of this couldn't be overstated. We laughed, unable to take the protest seriously despite its excellent and honorable intentions. They could've easily avoided this by protesting during the day, when the routes aren't linked. It's called a little bit of research, guys, we quipped to each other, giggling. Ruining bus service for black people in transit-dependent neighborhoods is prooooooobably not what they were hoping to accomplish... but buku brownie points for having their hearts in the right place!

After about 90 to 120 minutes of delays, depending on which of those six buses we're talking about, we all finally made it to the U-District. The coordinator was slammed with a high-level accident in Ballard and couldn't get back to us to direct us on how to return to schedule. Running all six buses in a row back to Rainier Beach would be pointless.

We decided to improvise. I like to think we did a bang-up job of using our initiative and spreading the service out. A couple of us

Nathan Vass

worked on the 49 part of the route for the time being, while another drove the full ordinary routing of the 49/7 through downtown; I and one other operator expressed ourselves to the south end to serve Rainier Valley as quickly as possible. He would fly all the way down to the bottom of the Valley and be the first northbound trip; I would be the first bus in *nearly two hours* to do a southbound trip from Little Saigon to Rainier Beach.

I recall thinking, Whoever gets out there first on Rainier Avenue is going to get *annihilated*. Aside from a mass overload, what passenger on this green earth is going to be happy, waiting *90 to 120* minutes for a bus that normally comes every fifteen? Whoever that poor soul of a driver is who gets out there first...

Only later did I realize: *I am going to be that operator.* I didn't plan it that way; it just happened. I happened to get to Twelfth and Jackson before anyone else did and saw the angry mob. Grab this bull by the horns, I told myself, and dive in. Anything else would be too easy. You were made for stuff like this.

These folks were furious.

They didn't have the tech access to know why the bus was late or what had been going on. They'd just been seething, for an hour plus. As a bus rider who's experienced egregious service disruptions, I could sympathize. You have to understand: the 7 is some of the best and most heavily used bus service in the county. It runs every ten minutes during the day and every fifteen at night 'til midnight, with twenty-four–hour service after that. A gap this long in service that busy is a seismic event.

Speak loudly, confidently, kindly—Thank you for waiting, thanks for your patience, I appreciate your patience tonight—while also explaining as succinctly as possible: big protest tonight, blocked all of us for a hour and uh half, biiiig protest up on the Hill, *Black Lives Matter* protest...

That got their attention.

What could they do? What can you do, when the cause of the delay has been a fervent and much-needed call to action for your rights as a citizen? You couldn't be angry about it. That wouldn't make any sense. You could complain, but your complaints would fall away like so much chaff in the breeze. The wind would die down a little all over again, at each new stop. Sails slackened.

"OH MAH GOD," Devin said when he saw me finally at Walker Street. Devin's terrific. He works security at Walgreens. He and I like to talk about our workout routines. We're about the same age and body type. As the bus pulled up, we both threw our hands in the air upon recognizing each other. I always drive with the dome light on, but especially tonight—I wanted them to know it was me as early as possible. They know me out here. Anything to deflate those sails tonight.

"OH MAH GOD," he said again. "THEY SENT THE RIGHT BUS DRIVER OUT FO' *THIS* RUN. 'Cause I was 'bout to cuss *the shit* outta this muhfuggah so bad..."

"Devin, *thanks*, man!"

"Oh, my God."

"I'm glad it was *you* standin' right here!"

"This th' ONLY driver they coulda sent," he told the bus. He just had to get his pent-up energy out. I love how it tumbled out as something positive. "Aw, shit! I been waitin' so long, I was so ready to cuss out WHOEVER it was. But ah couldn't! 'Cause it was *him*! This the best bus driver in all Seattle right here! I cain't cuss *him* out!"

"Devin, man," I said. "Love you, dude."

"Ah love you too, man!"

"Iss good to see you. It's been crazy tonight. They marched from downtown all the way to the mayor's house..."

With this and other similar interactions, we turned the night around. Grab the bull by the horns, and make it happen. It was exhilarating. Over the microphone, I continued to periodically explain and thank, explain and thank. I refused to accept fare. How could I charge these overtaxed souls in such a circumstance? A young man raised his eyebrows in grateful surprise. "Good lookin' out," he said.

Nathan Vass

The acknowledgment on both sides of that small exchange, making waves in each person's heart.

In eavesdropping on the conversations around me I was reminded, potently, of the weight of the issue. Dwayne, an educated man who knows Shakespeare, working swing shift at a hardware store. Yolanda has a law degree but works four entry-level service jobs. It's near midnight, and she'll miss valuable sleep—she gets up at 5 AM tomorrow. Someone saying they shop for groceries every month using the same $54 amount they've been allotted for years. A boy revealing to his friend there's not enough water in the house for him to shower that night.

His friend said, "Just wear your other drawers, bro! I know you got three drawers!"

The first boy laughed shyly, and the second tried to make him comfortable, revealing that his family uses toilet water to wash their socks and underwear.

Black lives do matter. Last Tuesday they mattered in North Seattle, and took place in South Seattle.

Her face had been living and struggling in the same great whirlwind you have, and all the while you resided somewhere in the back recesses of her mind, unforgotten.

TJANG, AGAIN

5/11/2018

A familiar face came into focus amongst the crowd. There she was: a middle-aged Vietnamese woman I've seen only a few times in as many years. Sometimes she'd be on the route with her daughter, or we'd talk about the bakery she works at. What was her name, again? I barely know this person, and yet... how is it, the way such glancing interactions can feel so special to us, moments no less formative than those we make with our oft-more–considered loved ones. Two strangers who glow for each other, appreciating each other's attitudes on life, whose places in the world are each comforted by the other's existence.

Incredibly, she remembered my name, though I think haven't seen her since she gave me a loaf of pumpkin bread in what, 2012. We shook hands with both hands, letting the moment hold, pushing against time. The sort of connection based on only a few prior meetings, but in some mysterious fashion enough to make this, our present, significant. Travelers will know what I mean; shake hands with a stranger on the other side of the world, and seeing them now again you're best friends. This was smaller in geography but not in feeling. Her face had been living and struggling in the same great whirlwind you have, and all the while you resided somewhere in the back recesses of her mind, unforgotten.

Her name would not return to me until after I'd gone home. Tjang. Absolutes are few in this life, but this is irrefutable: the positive impact we have will always be larger than we're ever aware.

I bet you knew that already, but I wanted to tell you anyway.

I wrote that more than three years ago and would later present it as a postcard gift to all my friends at my thirtieth birthday party. For me, it's one of the moments that encapsulate everything. It's why you won't find me working behind a desk, taking administrative positions for more pay, pursuing a more lucrative career in wedding photography, moving into training or supervision anytime soon; my job allows me the delicate, ephemeral, one-of-a-kind pleasure of having interactions like the above... *all day.*

Just over a week ago I saw her again. The time of day, place, direction—everything was different, but there she was. I stopped walking, and she did too. Our names flew off each other's lips this time and we hugged tightly—there was a freedom to this meeting in that I wasn't working.

Someone was with her this time, her mother maybe, and we smiled our hellos, asked after each other, but more generally just glowed at each other. We radiated. The words were simple, cross-lingual baby talk, kind but limited; the hug was what really spoke volumes, that and our eyes, each registering the knowledge and sameness of what the other felt. What did it mean? What can it mean?

Many things, perhaps, but at least this: there is goodness in this world, and it continues ever forward—quietly, humbly, and very brightly.

Nathan Vass

It seemed
all he could
do but say,
"You're better
than this."

DIFFERENT SIDES

2/5/2015

It was a conversation of carefully considered words, and not one I could take part in. Robert Peace, the African-American Yale graduate whose life was tragically cut short in 2011, once told his Caucasian friend Jeff Hobbs in private that "there are niggers, and there are brothers. Niggers just like to start shit. They don't value human interaction, let alone human life." All they care about is "acting hard. Fronting."

To which Jeff Hobbs said, "What about brothers?"

"A brother's like me," Peace replied. "He just wants to take care of his own and chill."

These remarks, which derive from Hobbs' book about the death of his close friend Peace, a molecular biochemist who sank into the drug trade, came to mind while listening to the following exchange, as two black men quietly sparred over their separate perspectives on ways of living. In an interesting reversal of expectations, Man 1 was the older of the two, around sixty-five, while Man 2 was a healthy twenty-eight or so, big-boned and tall.

Man 1: Thinkin' 'bout goin' home. What choo doin' tonight? Where you goin'?

Man 2: I'm goin' home, Old School.

Man 1: Why you goin' home already? You don' like makin' money?

Man 2: Wha'chu talkin' about now.

Man 1: Street corner. Make a hunnerd dollars tonight, two three four.

Man 2: I been through that. Parents from Chi-town, I'm from Warshington. [Meaning D.C.] I already been there, man. It's a waste of my time thinkin' about it.

Man 1: Man, whatchu know 'bout makin' money. "Waste of your time." Where you goin' das better?

Man 2: Said I'm goin home, to elevate my knee! I jus' had surgery, bro.

Man 1: Where you goin'?

Man 2: I already tol' you. Where you goin?

Man 1: Get my hustle on. You know.

Man 2: You ain't goin' home? Now you lyin'. Before you said you was goin' home, now you say you don't know. Now you say you hittin' the street.

Man 1: I don't need to go home, man.

Man 2: What? Everybody needs to go home. You gotta sleep."

Man 1: Don't need no sleep.

Man 2: Everybody needs sleep, Ol' School. You know what? I'm never gonna be like you.

Man 1: Wha' sat mean?

Man 2: I'm goin' up. Work. I'm goin' to the top, goin' to school. Goin' to class, Seattle Central College. I'm a work my way up there.

Man 1: You believe that? *Work* get you to the top? You believe that?

Man 2: That work pays off? Yeah! Not the kind you doin'. Whatever that is.

Man 1: Pssh.

Man 2: I ain't angry wit' choo, Ol' School. I'm not tryna raise no beef wit' you. I just curious. Why you ackin' up? Why you like dis?

Man 1: You don't know no older folks is all.

Man 2: Aw, it ain't that. I know plenny ol-school type a dudes. They happy! And, they sleep right now! To be happy you got to rest. Even a dog knows that.

There was a sobering melancholy in the second man's tone. He was critical but not hateful, less disdainful than disappointed that his fellow man wasn't living up to his full potential. It seemed all he could do but say, "You're better than this." Some people lament their lot and blame the world as the cause for their behavior.

Others look at the limited opportunities placed in front of them and wrest something out of them, taking control a step at a time, their can-do spirit building on itself, snowballing from a flickering whisper to an unstoppable force, reaping new dividends for themselves and others with each passing day; letting the momentum of their good character expand and solidify. As the second man left, I told him he was awesome, but I wanted to shake his hand, or laud him in some further way. He had a vision of the world as a better place, a place where things can be accomplished.

I admired him deeply for it.

I looked to
the driver,
to see how
he would
respond.

FOOTSTEPS TO FOLLOW

12/16/2016

I didn't understand what was going on. There were three passengers left. A silent young African-American man, possibly a UW student, or else just passing through the area. Fine. A white female passenger, silent as well, keeping to herself and her headphones. Also fine.

And then this guy, who was standing up now. A compact Asian fellow in a Raiders jacket, shouting in a deep bass voice. His face was blank of expression, but the gruff and throaty yells revealed a tightly wound presence within.

"Hey! Bus driver! Hey!"

"Hey!"

"I don't like how you are!"

There are certain comments I expect to hear because of the frequency with which they're spoken to me. This isn't one of them. I was more confused than anything else. "What's that?"

His face may have been as stoic as a mask asking for directions, but he was furious. He nearly made himself hoarse exclaiming the following:

"You invaded my personal fuckin' space! When I was getting on! I don't like when my personal fuckin' space is invaded, makes me fuckin' uncomfortable as shit! You waved your fuckin' paws in my fuckin' face when I was trying to pay the fuckin' fare! Fuckin' asshole, don't ever fuckin' do that fuckin' shit again! Waving your fuckin' paws all over my fuckin' face, right near my fuckin' head!"

Reader, I had, and have, absolutely no clue what he was referring to. I could summon utterly no memory of using my hands, or arms, to interfere with people's faces on this otherwise entirely docile trip to the U-District. There's the slightest chance he was paying the fare while I waved bye to someone exiting the back doors, but that would only be a concern if he had a personal bubble the size of Alaska. But never mind.

"Whoa," I said, respectfully. "I didn't mean to do that, man, I apologize."

"Don't ever fuckin' do that again makes me feel fuckin' uncomfortable! I don't like when people invade my personal fuckin' bubble! Fuckin' paws!"

"I apologize, man. I didn't mean to disrespect you."

"Fuckin' paws in my fuckin' face!"

Calmly: "I didn't mean no disrespect. I made a mistake. I made a mistake, and I appreciate you tellin' me what's up."

"Fuck."

"Thank you for lettin' me know. Not gonna do it again."

The only reason I reacted as I did, the only reason I knew to even try this approach, was because of something I saw on a bus in childhood. I was eleven, standing near the front. The driver, an older white man, had a sailor's cap on. His blue eyes twinkled as he nodded at the masses getting on at Bellevue Transit Center.

Nathan Vass

"You're an asshole," a young black man next to me told him, for no significant reason I can remember. I looked to the driver, to see how he would respond.

"Yup," the driver calmly replied in a quiet voice.

"No, you're the worst bus driver ever."

"Yes, you're right," the driver responded to the boy's continued tirade. He was getting past the moment, a duck's waxed feathers, moving beyond judgment and hurt; letting the boy get it all out at no loss to himself. Untouchable. Eventually the boy didn't know how to continue. You can cut down a stiff tree, but you can't cut down reeds blowing in the wind.

I was cowed into awe by the driver's patience and perspective. That's character, I thought. These are the great people I look up to. You don't see role models like that in the movies.

That old driver from so long ago, on the now-defunct 253, had no idea the great example he was setting, how much it resonated with me. I never spoke to him, after all. But for those thirty seconds, he was a teacher of mine. Twenty-odd years later, I'd put his lesson to use.

The woman with the headphones hadn't noticed a thing. She left, oblivious. But the African-American fellow, a few years younger than me, walked up to thank me before leaving. He didn't address the interaction, but I knew he'd watched it all. I'd seen him in the mirror. His eyes spoke more than his lips did, and he seemed to be processing, considering things. He nodded a deep respect to me as he stepped out. "Have a good night," he said. I wondered if he was seeing something not unlike what I once saw, decades ago.

Maybe we're all just paying it forward.

In moments like this you want to reach out to your fellow man, grab him by the hand or hug him tight...

"I LOVE EVERYBODY!"

10/20/2014

"Haaswundrinahcoul' haatransfergosheltuh," said the young boy in front of me. Which meant, "Hi, I was wondering if I could have a transfer to go the shelter?" He slurred it out in the same tonality as yesterday, eyes averted. A pudgy young thing in his late teens.

"Hey, I remember you from yesterday! Here you are. As long as you don't ask me that every day!"

He sheepishly bowed his head and scurried out of sight. I doubt very much he was homeless, what with his unmatted hair, clean skin, and new shoes—after a while you learn to thin-slice a person's economic condition pretty quickly—but as I've said before, I needed

---

The title comes from a high school graduation memory, which I remember with greater clarity than anything else about the event. Upon receiving the plaque on stage, a student I didn't know, overcome with joy, turned to the crowd, and, not knowing how else to express himself, yelled, "I love everybody!" I imagine the largeness of heart our former inmate experienced was something similar.

to give him the benefit of the doubt. What do I know? Maybe it'd only been a few days for him.

A few stops later, a tall man in clean clothes says, "I just got out of King County Jail." We're at Broadway and Roy, at the north end of trendy Capitol Hill, by Rom Mai Thai, Poppy, and the Deluxe, and definitely nowhere near any sort of prison facility. He's between thirty and forty, olive-skinned African-American mix, bald, with dark eyes and brows, like an Italian movie star. He speaks quietly, head tilted, hands outstretched in street sincerity.

I sigh inwardly, again. But that part of me is still there, the sympathetic unjudging good part of me which I hope I never lose. Out loud I say, "This is for you," handing him a transfer.

"*Thank* you," he says, with a truthfulness in his eye contact and timbre that's hard to fake. He pauses, the way you pause to thank someone who's saved your life.

He walks to the rear, tall and lanky and alone. I watch him in the mirror, way back there, going through his tiny bag of belongings. He unrolls a pair of jeans, stands, and changes his pants.

I'm beginning to believe.

He's trying to be modest, but there's nowhere else to do it. We're on an afternoon 49, populated with hipsters and students. You get to a state of living where shame is something you can no longer hide, and you just have to get on with the difficult business of inching forward. Who cares what these other people think? Can't afford the luxury of being able to do something about it. He stays generally out of their eyelines, putting on fresh clothes with an air of solitary preparation, keeping to himself.

At Campus Parkway a bunch of students gather their headphones and paraphernalia, preparing to exit. A girl readjusts her Coach purse, twisting her lipstick applier for an extra pucker. Meanwhile, he's walking back up to me. I smile at him through the mirror, seeing he wants to speak.

"Hey." Louder than a whisper, softer than conversation. "Thank you for helping me."

Instantly I know he's telling the truth. His tone of voice says it all. The fact that he walked all the way back up here says it all. In moments like this you want to reach out to your fellow man, grab him by the hand or hug him tight, just to let him know the world cares. There is a space for you that only you can fill, my friend.

"Oh, it's the least I could do. Congratulations, man, on getting out. Welcome back to the real world!"

He sighs heavily into a smile, letting go the burden weighing down his frame. "Thanks!"

"I'm so glad you got out. That's a big deal."

"I's in there sixty-nine days, man."

Don't ask about his crime, I think to myself. Not the point. "Too long! Well, not as long as some other guys, but anytime in there is too long,"

"I learned some valuable life lessons in there."

"Right on."

"And now it's time to..."

I know the sentiment he's about to express, and I preempt him by passing on words an ex-felon once earnestly told me: "This is Phase Two! It's a new phase, but it's still you!"

He looked at me. "Yeah, man!"

In those two words was a zeal I've never heard. I could see how the phrase resonated. In his voice was, well, love. Love for himself, for all the possibilities of goodness he possessed, that sensation of ebullient hugeness which fills you, where for a moment you see the belief your parents, your siblings and lovers, your ancestors had in you. You want to make real the greatness they saw, and you remember how beautiful the world has always been. A door is open, and for now, somehow, all things are new. He felt the goodness in him being acknowledged.

"Congratulations, man. It's a big deal. I admire that a lot." Referring to his spark. Let him ride that flash of insight forever. No wonder he didn't look like your typical inmate at the outset. He was humble, not overcompensating with bravado, nor was he broken or damaged of spirit.

Phase Two.

Thank you, my human cohorts, for proving wrong my assumptions, and righting my path of thinking.

I just like taking care of these things. Smoothing out the inconsistent details, rubbing the half-forgotten itches out of consciousness.

THINGS I'VE LEARNED FROM THE 358

3/1/2014

I've driven buses across the Aurora Bridge about a thousand times. Without fail, every time I do so, two thoughts cross my mind.

The first thought, inevitably, is how incredibly beautiful everything looks. Regardless of conditions, whether stormy, foggy, clear—whether a loamy yellow in the setting sun or night after dark in deep blues, where you can sense the vast space while hardly seeing it—Wow, I think, coming around the curve at Halliday and bursting into the wide open expanse.

It's absolutely gorgeous out here.

The second thought is always about Mark McLaughlin and Silas Cool, plunging off the bridge to their deaths, taking the bus and all the passengers with them. Perhaps you know of the incident; everyone on the bus either died or was injured, and the route number, then called the 359, was retired. Why change the number to the 358? As Ron Sims said in 1998, right after the event, "So that years from now, people will ask why? And we can remember a person we never want to forget."

As I cross the bridge where he died, driving the same route he drove, the question naturally occurs to me how I would feel if the same circumstances took place on my bus. Am I prepared for that, I always wonder. I know what the answer needs to be: I need to be completely okay with it, eyes open and ready.

We all have our differences, but there are a few universals. One of them, I think, is that we all wish to close our eyes for the last time having as few regrets as possible. People talk of squaring things away before they pass on. Time to make amends, as the saying goes. Having that long talk with your estranged brother; connecting with your daughter while there's still a chance. Being on good terms with the ones you love, and with yourself. But why wait till death's door to be able to look in the mirror?

There is a drive in me to be good, to try and make actual my ideal of a good person. This is reinforced by the daily reminder the Aurora Bridge offers. Awareness of death really means awareness of time.

We place value on time only because we know it is limited, and what Bruegel the Elder called the Triumph of Death can in fact be seen not as desolation but as a light, a gift of insight, the window through which we perceive the value of happiness and right action, now.

That's part of the drive in me to square things away. I like a clean closet.

John* found me when I first started on the 358 over a year ago, and was thrilled by my attitude. "This route is NO JOKE," he would say, amazed at the ebullient sensibility I chose to bring to the route. He'd stand at the front of the old 2300-series coaches and we'd gab it up.

---

* He of the white ponytail, the spry older man from "Ode to Aurora."

The bus was often full—the chat seat not available for him—and the yellow line he's supposed to stand behind was a couple feet back from my driver's seat, making it awkward for him to stand and talk to me while still following the rules. I wouldn't have minded if he were a bit over the line. But John would lean in precariously, positioning his body at a gravitationally suspect 45-degree angle, proudly pointing out how his feet were "definitely behind the yellow line, check it out," even if his entire body was in front of it. Clever guy. I enjoyed his company. He was rarely sober, coming from the bar after his day at work, and we would discuss the books he was reading, relationships, and kindness to strangers. I'd be riding the 44, a passenger, and I'd see him get on and we'd keep right on talking as if the intervening weeks or months hardly existed.

Then one night I was in conversation with a driver friend at Aurora Village Transit Center when he came over. I was keyed into the discussion I was having and intent on listening to my friend.

"Hey John," I said distractedly, happy to see him but anxious to keep talking.

"Hey, Nathan! How's it going?"

"Good, and you?"

"Good."

I smiled impatiently and he nodded, feeling uncomfortable in the ensuing silence. "Good to see you," I said quickly, and he strained out a polite smile and walked away. Immediately I regretted my standoffish attitude.

After that I didn't see John for a while, but I wanted to talk with him—erase that awkwardness and let him know that of course, I like his company. Yes, this is pretty small fry as far as regret-inducing dilemmas go, but sometimes it's the little things that gnaw at us.

Weeks later—there he was! At 85th Street outbound! Hooray! The crowd began filing in, face after face, but... no John. He stayed back, outside, choosing instead to wait for the next bus. "John, what the heck are you doing," I said aloud to no one in particular as I drove away. "You're supposed to be riding my bloody bus!"

On the second-to-last day that the 358 ever existed, I saw him again at 46th. My bus was packed, and the general consternation of people boarding and deboarding lasted several minutes. Once again he didn't board, instead standing just out of my sight, by the rear of the bus, sipping on his paper coffee cup.

"John! John, hey, man!" I said, jumping out of the coach and striding toward him. I didn't think about the crowd inside the bus, watching and waiting. I just needed to shake his hand. It would take too long to explain why. I just like taking care of these things. Smoothing out the inconsistent details, rubbing the half-forgotten itches out of consciousness.

"Oh, heeyy, Nathan!" he said, turning, becoming alive.

Me, grabbing his right hand in a firm shake, left arm reaching back for a man-hug. "What's goin' on, John? Good to see ya!"

"Hey, good to see you too!"

"How you been?"

"Oh, I've been great, I've been great, I'm just, you know..."

"You finishing up work?"

I honestly can't remember his response. I was too excited, gleaming as I took in his crisp eyes, chapped red skin, and bright smile.

"You wanna go for a ride?"

"Well, yeah, but, that thing is stuffed, man."

"Sure, sure."

"I think I'll finish my coffee here, get my book out."

"Sure no yeah, makes sense. You wanna relax, spread out on your way home, I'm into it."

"Yeah, you know."

"Hey listen John, always good to run into you."

"You too!"

"I'll see you again!" I said, hopping back inside my bus. We'd walked back up to the front together.

"Definitely!"

Only then did I register how odd all this must have looked to the other passengers. The last days of the 358* had the quality of time traveling at a speed outside my experience. The act of shaking John's hand collapsed the entirety of the day into a gesture. In it lived the desire to make things right, to touch the lives of all the strangers I'd come to know, to be close to the tough reality that had taken me in with such kindness... To live and breathe in these final moments, without the need to process them yet as memories, to learn how to glory in the last breath of time, without sadness.

---

* On Valentine's Day 2014, the 358 was permanently replaced by the E Line, identical in routing but different in temperament due to increased security and a more impersonal all-door boarding process.

All great things are predicated on a maybe.

YOU'VE BEEN A GOOD FRIEND OF MINE

7/15/2013

"Help me be strong," a man once said to another man.

"*Be* strong," the listener responded.

Don't ask me how bad her living situation was. You couldn't imagine it. The level of abuse she had no choice but to tolerate, the fast-food job that kept her out till the wee hours, and not in your favorite part of town. Bussing to and from for low wages, and caring for three young daughters all the while.

I paint this portrait not to elicit pity—she certainly had none for herself—but rather to celebrate the character of the person in question. She possessed a quiet, gentle resilience I found staggering. All this would be happening to her, and I'd see her on the bus and ask after her day; she possessed the herculean ability not just to smile, but to mean it. After getting to know her better, it was only more obvious her energy was genuine. "I'll work through it," she'd say, the wan smile often widening.

Her eyes twinkled with some unknown secret—belief in herself, perhaps.

She would course the flow of the world into a positive way, incredibly, with her own hidden potency. This is more impressive than it sounds; it means, in essence, that she was not reactive. Posturing works for some people, but not her. This woman, with her small frame and delicate features, was nobody's first idea of great strength, and her meek, observing demeanor didn't strike the mind as that of a go-getter. But never mind that. She is real, and this is her way; her gentle, unwavering spirit overwhelms our preconceived notions of what strength looks like. She got more done with a gesture than a lifetime of someone else's chest-thumping machismo.

In any event, her life had progressed to where she needed to escape her living situation. She'd tried to do so before and failed, to unspeakable physical abuse and emotional torture. We had become friends, but she'd fallen out of contact of late; here she is today, though, calling to tell me that yes, in fact, she was going to try to leave town again.

She'd almost made it the attempt previous, but today she'd made it as far as the train station, farther than before. She, her three girls, and a small amount of luggage, thanks to a friend of hers who risked a lot in helping—here she is now, and it could be possible, maybe, that they'll make it onto this train, just maybe, and the train will begin moving, before her abusers and controllers can find out and stop her... Maybe.

Just a few more hours.

I was just arriving at the base when she called. Could I stop by at the train station to say goodbye? I was almost at work. Time was running thin. Into the phone I told her, I just can't make it over there today. I have to go to work. I know it might be your last time here, but...

We knew each other once, she and I. A pessimist would argue that all life is an ongoing experience of continuous loss. Many other things happen in life, but pervasive loss is unavoidable. One com-

Nathan Vass

bats it only by finding closure in as many cases as one can. If you can find a way to say goodbye, do so. Because then you can sleep at night. I ruminated on this while staring out the window, communing with the skyscrapers and freeway overpasses: this can't be how it ends. She calls *one* person, me, to see her off at the train station, as she embarks on a new phase in her life free from the ugly suffering she's been made to endure—and I'm busy because I'm going to work.

No.

Metro's attendance policy is an unforgiving one: if I am one minute late to sign in for my shift, I'm not allowed to work that day. I don't get paid. On top of that, you get written up and disciplined for it. Your grace period is the fifty-nine remaining seconds of the minute that comprises your sign-in time. Was there enough time for me to get in my car, race to the train station, and race back?

All great things are predicated on a maybe.

I offer the rest of this story to the person in question, on the hope that you might, by incredible fortune, one day stumble across this:

Long hair tied back, with strands blowing in the wind. Blond wisps quivering with life. What do we do when a moment is too large to process? You feel the size of life, pulsing past with immediacy.

Sunlight slanting down on cement and brick facades, coloring it all with light and shadow; you're much thinner now, more than I've ever seen, a casualty of stress and a draining life. You haven't slept, or eaten. No makeup on today, and I don't think I've seen you more haggard, or more beautiful. I can hardly believe it, but even after all this, your smile is still there. The resilience enmeshed in the core of your being, a positivity that doesn't insist on itself. It's easy for you to be who you are, and maybe this is why your rich, bright smile burgeons forth now in the afternoon light.

The children play around you, blurs of movement, noise, and stillness. You feel it in the air: the quality of a memory, here and now, the sensation of being steeped in the history of passing time, even as it all takes place.

There is something that money, education, culture, and status lead us away from, make us forget: it is ineffable, but it is related to the importance of truth and quiet conscience, of being happy. For you this is easy to embody. I'm not worried about you; just curious to know what'll happen next.

This is her time, I thought, walking out to my bus, having made it—incredibly—back to work on time. No one will know of her decency. She will never be famous for it, but in my mind I'm thinking, these are the heroes of our age. These are the faces I want to see on billboards. Puffy white clouds drift apart in the vast blue dome, letting the warm rays shine a little warmer. Just an ordinary beautiful Seattle afternoon for so many people, but for our friend on that train—yes, it was moving now—worlds had shifted. For her, looking out at the sliding landscape, factories and warehouses and the glinting sea, today is the beginning of another universe. Freedom.

It was a fleeting five minutes, over almost before it happened, but long enough for a tight hug and change of hands, and a look following a kiss I won't forget. No pictures were taken, no moment lasted long enough... but there was an effervescence to it all, where the rich, full weight of having known each other invested the passing seconds with something real.

In stories the climactic moments are grand. In life they are small, and they pass by before we can grasp them. You marvel at the speed and texture of existence in such moments, where time moves differently. I don't know if I felt sad or happy or what else, standing there with her. It was the experience of being at the forefront of life, in that space before emotion and processing—nothing other than the rushing, unadorned present.

When the energy is heavy, and the light is low, I hope you hear it. It's there, in the quiet hours of the night. A voice, a word, a whisper:

You've been a good friend of mine.

Nathan Vass

Continents,
ethnicity,
histories,
and oceans
meant
nothing
to them.

THE HUG

5/27/2017

Is she French? Italian, Eastern European? I don't know. I can never make out the words when they're speaking, she and her daughter.

Here she is today, forty maybe, with short hair, in a lavender turtleneck and shades perched up above her forehead. She has that refined sensibility you can't fake without overdoing it, the steady poise that lives on the other side of the Atlantic. Her expressive brown eyes smile with pride at her young daughter, a girl of perhaps eight whom she's picked up, as usual, from gymnastics class. They smile together, separated by decades but linked by love and blood.

Now, a boy running on, followed by his young father. The little force of nature bounding in between other passengers, holding something like a Nintendo DS in hand but equally excited by all around him. He squeals with delight. Dad's behind him, smiling at me as we laugh at each other in understanding. Kids. It's a good thing.

Father and son are dressed alike, you could almost say matching: fresh, flat-billed baseball hat with cornrows peeking out underneath, black felt street jacket over a black and umber sports jersey, dark jeans and basketball shoes, glossy with the thick white laces. Be black and be proud, Malcolm X said. They had the loudness and rhythm and chaotic colorful verve I call American.

With age we forget how to transcend race. The little boy ran over to the little girl. Continents, ethnicity, histories, and oceans meant nothing to them. They briefly stared at each other like puppies in love, and then you'd guess they'd always been fast friends, the way they're playing now, he a little younger than she. He's squeezing into the seat where she's sitting, showing her the game he's playing, the two of them talking and smiling with their big eyes and baby cheeks.

I watched the mom and the dad. He stood in the aisle next to her, and they followed in the lead of their respective children, talking and smiling, laughing in the shared act of parenting, a lifestyle you treasure even when you lament it. Sure, their conviviality required a touch more effort, but it was no less magical to witness. It was happening. They may have been the two least similar people on the bus then, in dress, temperament, and origin, but I know what they were thinking as they watched their children play.

We have a lot in common.

When it was time for mom and daughter to leave, she thanked the young man for his company—nice to meet you—and he responded with enthusiastic fervor. He reached an arm around her in an awkward hug. The space in the aisle, his other hand holding toddler stuff, the moving bus—it was uncoordinated, inelegant... and absolutely magnificent.

It didn't matter the awkwardness. I could see that he wanted to, needed to. The equal plane, convivial with such a seemingly different person, being spoken to not through the context of race but from the wider commonality of personhood. In her eyes, he lived as a good man. He was just another responsible parent.

The interaction had meant the world, and it was important to him to say so.

None of us
can completely
imagine the
sensation
that man was
describing
about himself.

ONE DAY, MY FRIEND

4/18/2015

Some years ago I directed a short narrative film called *As They Rise*, which stars the great Ryan Cooper. He was playing a recently homeless man undergoing a shift in his way of thinking. At one point during the shoot we were working underneath the Alaskan Way viaduct (the now-extinct section where the elevated portion lowered down to the ground), getting some B-roll of Ryan walking around in various dilapidated environments.

It was a surprise when, amidst shooting, an actual homeless person came over to have a few words with him. The man, a grungy sort in his fifties, had been observing and quickly intuited what we were trying to replicate. He went over to Ryan and spoke in low but earnest tones. I've never forgotten what he said, which was, "You're not doing it right. You have to put your head in the space of, you have *nothing* to look forward to. You have absolutely *nothing* to look forward to, to bring you up. There's no hope, no possibility, nothing. There is just this, right here."

Now, Ryan is a very focused, dedicated actor who puts a lot of consideration into how he performs the text—just the type of actor I like working with. I would expect an amateur to miscalculate the actuality of homelessness. But for someone of Ryan's professional caliber to still not quite have it down was a wake-up call. None of us can completely imagine the sensation that man was describing about himself—the feeling of treading water, quite possibly forever.

Ryan took the instruction well, and the man's words led to an improvement in the performance. I remember turning to Brian Bell, our AD, and quipping, "This guy gives better direction than I do!"

Half a decade later I was driving the 44 when I saw Avery catnapping on the bus stop bench at inbound Phinney. Avery is not the homeless man in the above narrative, but he is of the same condition. I knew him before he was homeless. He once worked at the Greenwood library, then at Dexter Horton, then at *Real Change*, until all was reduced to the disappointed present, a spot on a bench, then a bus, then the backside of a building, ever moving, never welcome.

But I'd known that face before the layers of comfort faded. He used to ride my 5, proactively greeting the passengers along with me and volunteering to help with heavy bags. He was so helpful I had to ask him to tone it down a little. The guy was too good at doing too much of my job!

I've never asked what caused his downfall. My friend Stephanie and I were recently discussing a woman we saw slumped over on the sidewalk one midnight in Jackson Park. "What are you thinking?" I asked Stephanie, after we'd driven past in silence.

She said, "I was thinking, it must be very cold for her. And that maybe she's hunched over like that because she's been sitting there for sixteen hours and she can't help but start falling asleep. Then I thought, maybe she's hunched over because she's incredibly high on some kind of drug and she can't even feel the cold."

"True. That's possible."

"But then I thought, why does it matter which one it is? Why should that change how I feel about her? Isn't it still bad that she's out there?"

Better put than I could have said. I let Avery keep his reasons to himself. We all make poor decisions, or find ourselves victims of other poor decisions. I simply called out his name that day, letting out a big wave, hand straight up in victory mode. He recognized me instantly and put himself together, different parts of his body coming to life, getting out of his cramped, slouching intermittent slumber.

"Avery! I didn't mean to wake you up or nothin'—"

"Oh hey, no! I will not hold you up, but I had to say, it is *good* to see you!"

"Aw man Avery, it's good to see *you!*"

"All love, brother."

"All love!"

"How you been?"

"Always good, man, always good!" He replied. "And you?"

"Beautiful as always!"

"That's right!" he exclaimed. To me, to himself.

"Thanks for sayin' hey, man. Hope I see you around!"

"I'll be out here!"

"You and me both, man! I'll be lookin' for you!"

My heart surged as I drove away. I felt so proud to know this man's name. He may be of the same condition as the man who approached our film set, but he is not of the same cloth. Avery still has hope. He has something motivating him, something forged deep within, and it bubbles to the surface when I catch his eye. Every time I find him I ask after his welfare, and even if things are clearly terrible, he'll shrug it off, calling it a phase, reminding himself he has control over the situation.

One day I'll see you with clean clothes and a haircut, my friend, and you'll tell me about some new job you like. And we'll laugh about how it was before, laugh about the times we've made, laugh like we did before the future came to be, talking on the 5 and saying hi to everyone. You're out there somewhere, right this minute. I believe in you.

The earth has orbited just about once, and I've been distracted with my own day-to-day life, but this man has been otherwise occupied.

JUST ABOUT ONE ROTATION

10/18/2013

Upon reaching home I fished the keys out of my pocket, looking at the door handle of my apartment. I noted the evening sunlight caressing the door's wooden surface, and I paused.

A face from earlier jogged itself in my memory. I realized that a passenger I greeted today on my bus was the same man I wrote about last winter. At the time* I had described him thus:

Another fellow, a middle-aged white homeless man, his face utterly destroyed, beaten to a pulp. The skin has turned black, and the cuts on the eyebrows are drying. He's lost his backpack with his HIV paperwork and his last $100. Tough-looking character, but his voice is human. I can't tell if he's crying.

---

* From "Ode to Aurora."

I stood outside my home for a moment longer, registering the incredible fact that this man is still alive.

Having witnessed his earlier state up close, it seemed to me nigh impossible. I realized the only commonality in his appearance between now and then was his sharp blue eyes, though today they were dry. If anything, he actually looked younger now. I would never think to describe him as middle-aged. The man's regressed at least ten years.

Today his skin was long since healed, no scars I could notice, and he had fresh clothes and a smile to go with them. The earth has orbited just about once, and I've been distracted with my own day-to-day life, but this man has been otherwise occupied. He has forced himself back up from the ashes. I imagine no one else on my bus today knew of the travails he had undergone; certainly they didn't know what he looked or sounded like one day last winter. It took me several hours to put together where I'd seen that face before.

I am humbled into a quiet state of awe.

I breathed in, feeling the words travel down, the memories behind them, as they slid to the pit of my stomach.

LEAVE THE QUESTIONS

5/9/2018

Stories come out slowly sometimes, awkwardly. They belch and burp their way forth. This young man approached from the bus's crowded interior with a hesitance, standing by me as I drove, no reason given. I thought he was about to jump off. He wasn't. He just watched me, keeping to the side, while I greeted and fared the people well, wrapping the wheel around the corners, accents and smiles bouncing off me as I registered his gaze nearby. What was he thinking, beneath that knit beanie? Behind the dirty off-gray sweatshirt with the high-school logo, the army camo fatigues tied round at the bottom, the better to display his basketball socks and shoes? Finally I just went for it.

"How's it been goin'?"

"Iss coo'," he replied, in a monotone I took to be standard-issue emotionless male adolescent, but which quickly revealed itself to be something more. "I was just in this accident though. The driver died."

"Aoouuugh," I said. He was young. Should a high-schooler know the face of death this well? "I'm so sorry. Somebody you knew?"

I wasn't looking at his face, but it felt like I was, hearing the naked grit in his voice: "Mah best friend."

"Aaaooo," I moaned again. "I am so sorry. I know how that feels."

"And he was a good guy too, he had a job, just turned twenty-six. He the type a guy he'd give you his last five dollars, you know?"

I breathed in, feeling the words travel down, the memories behind them, as they slid to the pit of my stomach. Let yourself go there, I thought. A positive worldview should be able to tolerate anything. What is optimism? Optimism is being comfortable looking at truth, even if it's negative. I don't understand how this place works, but I like living here. Life may be unfair, but people don't have to be. What are we here for, if not to help our fellow man through a spot of hardship? I felt his burden too, and tried to share it with words.

"Oh my gosh, that's heavy," I said. "I know what you mean though. It's the best people I know, that die young. I don't understand it."

"Yeah."

"I guess all we can do is keep that person's good spirit alive, let 'em live through our actions." I meant it, but it sounded false, the comforts you're not ready to hear in the days after.

We were facing the mystery around which religions are built, ideologies and philosophies, the one question no amount of millennia can conclusively answer: *Why do bad things happen to good people?* It's the humanized condensation of yet a larger query. You've asked it even if you don't think you have. *Why does order in the universe seem present sometimes and absent at others?*

Most human thought stems from this question, and it is our nature to ask it, no matter how smartly the ol' universe keeps its secrets. We know we can never know, are not allowed to know, and yet... Sure, he was a husky macho man of a teenager, but I knew the question lived in his mind also. The doubt.

I found myself saying, "Yeah, 'cause I used to think you know when I was little, if you're a good person, then you're gonna live a long time. And it just ain't true. At all."

"It's almost like it's the opposite," he murmured.

"Or something."

Do actions have consequences?

"I think when it's your time, it's your time."

"Yeah. That makes sense." I nodded again. I'll take the suggestion of order, even if I can't comprehend it. "That makes sense."

Maybe it's not about consequences. Maybe it's acting *qua* acting, for the sake of itself, how it makes you feel... for the good it does you and others. Maybe that is its own reward. I mused: "The thing is, I still wanna be a good dude. Even if I don't live a long time, I wanna feel good about the stuff I do in this life, you know?"

"Yeah. I think it's like God givin' me a second chance."

"Yeah, an opportunity." I looked at his cast. "How's your hand?"

He mentioned pain pills, numbness, two more months of the cast. I said something about how that's better than a wheelchair. He said yeah. He opened up as the bus emptied out; just us now.

There were three others in the car, he explained. His best friend, his girlfriend, and his best friend's girlfriend. One girl broke both her legs, and the other her ribs. His friend the driver gone. It went unspoken who made out the best.

Our friend's lasting problem is not a physical injury but a psychological one, a roiling storm he will likely never manage to convey to others who haven't also experienced similar catastrophes. He will know the force of the questions above with a slamming weight unique to him, and the resulting loneliness will inform his every thought and action to a degree even he won't be able to wrap his mind around. It will be this haze, the invisible suffering that gives him the long view, but keeps him forever distant.

There is a type of grief where you have no tears left. You can't cry; you've run out. It sounds like you don't care, but you're just hoarse from a passion too big for your voice. That's where our boy was. We were at the terminal, standing outside the bus now. I listened as he reflected. "We were going to the Paradise Restaurant. Just goin' to get something to eat. I guess he went to the real paradise." Pause. "And he was just twenty-six, such a good guy. Like ah said, he the type he'd give you his last five dollars if you needed it."

"That's such a good age too, I mean you're all done with school, you're a new adult finally doing something with your life, got all kinds a possibilities..."

"Dude, yeah. Man, I have nightmares every night. We used to see each other every day. Now, it's like this...?"

There's not much you can say after that. We ended on a note of God bless, genuine thankfulness at being alive. I watched him stalk away, another young man in a beanie, doing his best at the extraordinary challenge and seemingly nigh-impossible game we call Living Life.

What cures you from the knowledge of the shape of the Void? What pulls you back? Will there be a day with enough hindsight behind it, when a sunrise is a sunrise again, and the questions don't need answers anymore?

One day, he will know. And I think he will smile.

When life has thrown certain obstacles your way in the past, being thankful becomes a hard-earned habit.

LAUGH LINES

1/31/2014

"Well, look who it is!" Carlos yelled to me recently, overjoyed at 6:02 AM, eastbound on Jackson. He was on his way to work.

Carlos and I have talked before. He is tall and thin, with one of those faces that creases easily into a smile. Somewhere in his fifties, with dark almond eyes and a strong baritone voice.

He had recently fallen into some incredibly good fortune; after struggling to survive for some time, Carlos was able to land a construction job through an acquaintance, and proved himself through hard work. The gig required skill sets in all areas, which he possessed—siding, plumbing, roofing, installation. Years of odd jobs were paying off now, and he was finally getting an *outstanding* hourly wage—higher than my own at the time. I was thrilled to hear it, though I couldn't help but silently wonder how long this would last.

Didn't opportunities this good always have a catch? Would he be able to keep up with the demands of the job? Would the bosses be fair? Would the work continue? Carlos marveled at his good fortune, and neither of us could believe how great it all sounded. But as the weeks and months progressed, he was still there.

Sometimes there is no catch.

That big smile on his face, exhausted but exceedingly happy at the day's end. It's all in your attitude. When life has thrown certain obstacles your way in the past, being thankful becomes a hard-earned habit. His laugh lines were more soul-stirring to me than any number of perfectly made-up faces.

Some months later, I recall riding a driver friend's bus one afternoon. Riding your friends' buses may not sound fun, but it is. At what other job can you visit your friend and gab with them for an hour or two—or more? I'd chat with Brian, one of the great titans, talking film and philosophy on Beacon Avenue. When things were busy I'd watch and learn from his style of working, or wander a few seats back to answer phone calls. A comfortable environment.

Personalities come and go in this city. In the wee hours you'll look up at the ceiling, wondering whatever happened to that lonely soul who used to show up every morning on your route. I hadn't seen Carlos in a while, when—there he was, just now, walking past me on Brian's 36, going to the back to chat with an acquaintance. I followed him back there, curious to hear how he was doing.

"Same as ever," he belted out ebulliently, proudly showing me pictures on his phone of what he was working on. I saw plumbing fixtures, scaffolding, empty rooms. I saw his crow's feet laughing out. The work wasn't lagging at all—his boss was starting in on nine apartment buildings, tearing them all down and rebuilding them. Carlos' wages had stayed the same, the working conditions were fair, the shift bosses were excellent, and his supervisor had even promised him an apartment in one of the completed buildings, if he so chose. "Wow," I said. Internally I was once again skeptical. But, so far, so good.

Months after *that* meeting, and it's now me driving the 36, putting to use what I observed in Brian and other stellar operators,

Nathan Vass

while throwing in my own spin on things. It's 6:02, approaching Jackson and 12th—

"Well, look who it is!"

Is everything still going great? Yes. Carlos exuded a bursting positive energy, bringing up everyone around him without even trying. All at once polite, present, and street. I asked him how things were going. His answer was no different than in the months previous. He's thrilled to be here. "That's so great," I said, silently thinking: With an outlook like yours, Carlos, I'm not surprised!

"That's so fantastic," I continued, speaking partly to him and the rest to myself.

"I don't understand it, to be honest. Sometimes this shit just happens," he said loudly, looking out at the predawn sky, unable to hide a smile.

Time is what
makes the
details build
on each other,
stories the
journey, etches
into space
the gradual,
layered nature
of existence.

LOVE, DEEPLY

9/27/2017

They got on in true ragtag fashion, a duo right out of Dickens, dressed in black and cluttered flair, clutching mysterious bags in one hand while reaching to balance the rest of their gear with the other. The outfit of the street person can't be faked, or at least not very well, because its principle ingredient is time. Time is what makes the details build on each other, stories the journey, etches into space the gradual, layered nature of existence. These two souls were no fakes.

I noted her pale and weathered skin, a blotchy beige on her arms—not unattractive actually, but rather a record of a lot of life lived. Her amiable rasp of a voice, which told you: here is a woman who's been to all fifty states. She had to be around the half-century mark, and he several years her senior. His complexion, ruddy and textured, spoke similarly, a big-boned lifetime of adventures high and low.

You can sense when couples have been together a long time. A similarity in dress, perhaps, or a consistency in body language; the complimentary understanding of years spent filling spaces jointly, a casual two-step deeper than dance. Few things are more gratifying than seeing the passage of significant time together writ affably upon spouses or partners. It's impossible to manufacture, and quite rare.

That's precisely the energy these two were putting out. They were both attired in black jeans, black shirts, black shoes, clean but tattered; tattoos peeking out from her faded blouse, bracelets and rings, a modest wedding ring on the appropriate finger. He with his silver-streaked ponytail, skin that seemed at various times equal parts tanned and burned, a string necklace holding something special.

They glowed.

They were clearly exhausted, but exhausted together; whatever their challenges, they faced them not between each other but as a unit, looking outward. She sorted something out among their belongings, encouraging him to rest, shortly before doing the same, leaning her head against his.

I wasn't driving this time, but riding, just another passenger seated behind them. Her presence struck me so; I realized I'd seen her before. That fun shock of dyed blonde hair, and the kindness; yes, now I remember. A fleeting moment on a summer night in 2014, wherein she exchanged wisdom about love and loss with words I continue to go back to.* Today, now, I didn't need to interrupt them. They catnapped as one, drifting in and out of wakefulness, swaying to the gentle rhythms of the long freeway drive.

Finally he spoke to her, softly. "You're the best woman in all the wide world," he said, his bass-heavy gravel voice tender. "And the best thing that's ever happened to me."

She smiled, eyes still closed, nudging her head closer.

---

* Rachel, from "For the Sake of the Others."

Nathan Vass

You are that memory that drifts in on a rainy day, in the midst of a cluttered market, on the beach alone.

ANDY AFTER DEATH

9/26/2013

There was a face I saw regularly a couple of years ago. He was a regular at Rainier and Dearborn, northwest corner; the fellow with one arm and one front tooth, dressed in soiled black rags right out of Dostoyevsky.

He had strong, clearly defined features, a face battered by life and apparently all the happier for it. Funny, how a smile can transform one's being. He was liked not because he was attractive, but because he was always beaming. Confidence. Whenever he saw me, he would practically explode with delight, and I would do the same. My passengers on the 7 would smile.

Once, two frat boys gave him a Big Gulp filled with motor oil, as a cruel joke; he was in the emergency room all night as a result, but afterwards was still as positive as ever. Talk about a resilient worldview. If he can be happy, I have no excuse. These guys are pros.

For me it was important to get a wave in. Who knew how hard his day was progressing? Maybe that small gesture—actually, a rather large one, as our waves, complete with fistpounds to our sternums and peace-sign salutes, were massive—was sorely needed. I recall a day when I was in my car driving past; he didn't see me, and I didn't stop because I had no food on offer. But I did have my emergency gallon water jug. Did his thirst qualify as an emergency? Yes.

I U-turned round and peeled back, stopping at a red across the street. He recognized me in my non-bus car and street clothes, as I ran across the lanes with the gallon of water. The day was a scorcher, and he really needed it.

"Thanks so much for that day, bro," he would tell me so many times afterward. "I still got the jug as a keepsake!"

Often there was a second man panhandling there—a quieter fellow, mild in both manner and look. They'd amble amongst different sets of cars looking for handouts, not quite stepping on each other's turf. Time went by and the day came when I noticed I hadn't seen the Dostoyevsky guy in some time.

I asked Mild Guy about it.

"Hey, where's the other guy? I haven't seen him in a while."

"Oh, Andy? He's dead."

"*What?*"

"Yeah, he died a couple months ago."

"What? Oh, my goodness. I haven't been on this route for a bit."

"Yeah. He didn't take very good care of himself."

"Shoot. That's a shame. What a great attitude that guy had."

"Yeah, he was cool."

Today, more than a year later, I look over at the northwest corner of Rainier and Dearborn, minding my own business—double take. There's a figure over there, dressed almost exactly as Andy always was, except this guy is younger, and he's breakdancing. Andy had a severe limp and a missing arm; he could never move this fast. But otherwise the resemblance—specifically the wardrobe—is uncanny; I don't know if it's an intentional tribute or not. It is for me. It's as if Andy's ghost is still dancing, moving and breathing as he never could in life. A blur, pinwheeling in and out of himself, that smile transformed into movement, a ball of energy rising, a revolving top, a whirling dervish...

How do we exist after death? In the memories of others. We live in their minds, as long as they remember us. We carry on in their hearts and actions, informing their thoughts. You are that memory that drifts in on a rainy day, in the midst of a cluttered market, on the beach alone. You spread and multiply, many different places at once, your friends and lovers taking a second glance at that bookshelf, or laughing at something you always did, or them sticking up for something because they distantly remember your attitude, defiantly positive to the end.

Then you fade away.

Smaller and smaller inside all of them, becoming more a part of them than an identifiable memory of you. You spread into the soil of the human spirit, no longer a corpse but now everywhere and nowhere. You were a person, then a memory, then an idea, then a feeling, then everything.

I can still see him now.

Do you
remember
what it
was to ride
the bus
as a child?

AFTERWORD

7/2/2017

That's me in the previous picture at left, at thirteen or fifteen years of age, sitting behind the wheel of a 4000 in the Atlantic Base yard. What was I thinking about, in eighth grade? I'm wearing a green Old Navy fleece there, new at the time. It still fits me.

July 2nd, 2017, marked for me ten years to the day of bus driving. A decade earlier on a Monday afternoon I took out a (now defunct) 250 from Bellevue Base and drove it from Seattle to Redmond. The entire shift was two hours and twenty minutes, the fare was just over a dollar, and though the route went on the freeway I doubt I once went over forty-five miles an hour.

My father took the photograph to the right, which dates from later that week. I'll never be able to express the level of gratitude I have for him taking the time to come out and surprise me with a ride, documenting it with the family camera. This wasn't just another job. It was the culmination of a lifelong passion.

Hang on, you're thinking. *A lifelong passion?* What? From some-one who ran a wedding photography business, got multiple films into festivals, traveled the world, and has had thirty-odd art shows?

Let me explain.

Sometimes we love quickly, without knowing why; or the reasons change across the years, even if the feeling remains.

Do you remember what it was to ride the bus as a child?

There was no pop culture in our home growing up: there were books aplenty but no TV, magazines, radio, newspapers, or films... Secondary and tertiary representations were minimized in favor of pure, unadulterated direct experience. I was filled with a hunger insatiable for being close to life; give me that which is tactile, au-thentic, unadorned. Take me to the leading edge.

I went through a phase where I'd borrow my father's bus pass. It represented a level of freedom analogous to a library card, only this knowledge was firsthand. I rode all over town. At twelve I branched out of the 'burbs and began riding into Seattle alone—sometimes with the camera, but often with just my eyes. I quickly discovered the journeys were frequently more interesting than the destinations.

Woody Allen once wrote that a city, because of its complexity, could never fully be captured in a work of art; there's just too much detail, too many moving parts. It was this variegated complexity that thrilled me so. I was a shy child, more observer than partici-pant, and observe I did, in every corner of the metropolis. Our city is well-suited for this; Seattle's neighborhoods are stark contrasts to each other, self-enclosed enclaves of income level and ethnicity. It reminded me of L.A., this place that reveals itself in layers. The more time you spend in the Emerald City, the more you discover.

I rode through the safest parts of town, and more often through exactly the opposite; I was too unobtrusive to invite much notice in such areas. There was more verve and color out here (not to mention better bus service), where lives were not so sequestered from each other, and compassion carried greater currency. Certain images have burned themselves into my memory:

Nathan Vass

- The early morning 7 runs carrying the blind workers down Rainier Avenue; I smiled in the darkness, listening to their jovial banter. They lit up the night.
- Elsewhere, a young Indian housewife vomiting silently into a paper bag, upset by the driver's careless starts and stops. She kept to herself, demure and uncomplaining.
- The memory outlined in "Footsteps to Follow."

I watched people help each other, or avoid doing so. I saw the smiles of runners who made the bus, and felt the disappointment when I missed a connection. People went out on the town; they came home from work.

The older coaches in use had a different character than the newer equipment we see now. Evidence of time was everywhere—faded metal, peeling paint, vandalism, the smells of decades past. Seats were designed for appeal and comfort, not cost savings. You looked out through scratched windows at history, advancing and receding with each new block. Nothing was computer controlled; the texture of sounds was different. We were in the era before hums and beeps. One rather heard the pressure release of opening doors, oiled joints creaking, the snap of switching wire; mechanical parts sliding against each other, dynamic brakes and engine retarders singing their fluid song. Everything was real.

All this to say, that amongst the beautiful life with my parents, and the world of school and friends, I found comfort in this vast human maelstrom. In time, as adolescence and adulthood drew nigh, joyriding through the city got pushed aside in favor of other concerns... but how could I forget those formative days?

So many turning lives, such incredible detail, everywhere. The bus came to represent for me something very different than what I imagine it means for others. My classmates knew humanity through their friends and parents. I knew it through those avenues, but also through the journeys of the untold thousands, faces and lives I'd seen up close, strangers behaving just as I do, loving, breathing, laughing, and dying, commonalities crossing over age and language, culture and status. I could never bully anyone now; I'd seen too much of the lives of strangers to consider anyone the "other."

A fundamental truth emerged, and I didn't know its name until years later: I am surrounded by friends, and I share some common ground with every person on this planet.

The primary sensation I have today, upon reflection, is gratitude. These folks have taken me in, accepted my enthusiasm and the currency of respect. A man on last night's 7 asked how everything was in my life.

"Good, it's been good," I replied. "We just had the shakeup and all the other drivers picked new stuff, but I stayed right here, man, same time same hours, same days,"

"You like this number 7, huh?"

"I know too many of the folks to leave!"

He grinned. "You one of us, man. You part of the 'hood now!"

I never guessed it could turn out like this. My art career means a lot to me, but so too is there something special about all this bus stuff. I felt like an anomaly as a child. I imagine most of us do. But now, to be appreciated on this level, by the masses who I grew up riding with and the masses who read these stories here and elsewhere, who care about kindness and positivity and the human element of urban life... I always thought my perspective was a minority one. I'm so thankful to discover how many of you loving people there really are.

Thanks for reading and riding!

Acknowledgments

There's an interesting thing that happens during awards shows. You've noticed it while watching them. The winners get up there, and rather than deliver what everyone wants to hear—a compelling speech—they instead reel off a list of names of those who helped them get where they are. As a viewer, it's profoundly boring.

But after receiving rather more accolades than I know I deserve, I know now why they do that.

They do it because when you're in the position of being honored for your creative pursuits, you know, utterly, that there's no way any of this happened through your efforts alone. It's always by the grace of fate and the goodness of your compatriots. Your gratitude for those beautiful people overwhelms, and no amount of showered compliments can accurately express what you're really trying to tell them: *None of this would be happening without you.*

That's how I feel about the list of names below. Any words I summon here will be inadequate. I'll settle for stating the fact that they are the true authors of this book, in that they inspired me, taught me, pushed me, and helped me. Of them as much the people in the stories themselves, I am at best a vessel and an amalgamation.

This is really Tom Eykemans' book. I can't take credit for its existence. It was he, not I, who originally broached the idea, birthing it out of the morass of notions we creatives daily throw at our private walls; who shepherded it into reality with his enthusiasm, creativity, and force of will. I'm too busy writing the stories (not to mention driving the bus!) to concurrently plumb the myriad details of bookmaking with his customary level of finesse, care, and design.

My gratitude goes to Tom Eykemans, for approaching me. For his design, ideas, loyal enthusiasm, and support. And to Jacqueline Volin, for her editing. I imagine she receives the term "eagle-eyed" as a compliment often; her proofs, with their detail and suggestions (and impeccable handwriting) are art pieces in their own right. (These two knew each other as colleagues before they knew me. Jacqueline would later learn that the driver whose blog Tom read also happened to be the driver who drove her home while talking to her about the *New Yorker* articles they were both reading. At some point, each of us knew the other without knowing the third was also known to them. Years later we three would all be collaborating on this project!)

Thank you also to Charles Mudede, for lending your words to our cause; Paul Constant, for your generosity of spirit, on evidence in your thoughtful interview; Paul Currington, for allowing art to happen, making time and space and reflection; Rachel Randall, Leroy Haigler, Miranda Wright, Brian Jobe, Laura Hamje, Avery Nelson, and others, for sharing and so much more; Quinn Hallenbeck, critically; Donald and Esther Vass, for reacting to the stories and assisting with selection, structure, and title; Brittany Hammer, for further considering and ruminating; the lovelies at Girlie Press, for your precision and care; Eric Myers, for being gracious; Jenine Lillian, for living up to your name of catalyst; Miriam Kolker, for brainstorming titles over a late-night barroom table.

And to you, the downtrodden, the undesirables, the forgotten people who caress the city like invisible drops of rain. You are not invisible to me. This is how I see you, my friends, with these lines; you, who accepted me into your community when you didn't have to. You were nice to the skinny guy in the button-up shirt and glasses, who was so friendly it didn't make sense. Understand the compliment in my calling you a muse, the respect I wish to extend in calling you a mirror.

Show this book to the ones who think you have no name.

For M & B

Library of Congress Control Number: 2020941354
ISBN: 978-1-63405-015-9

Chin Music Press
Seattle, Washington
www.chinmusicpress.com

Design by Thomas Eykemans
Typeset in Georgia and Helvetica
Proofread by Jacqueline Volin
Printed and bound in Canada by Friesens

A version of the introduction, entitled "Talking with Seattle's blogging bus driver,
Nathan Vass," was originally published by the *Seattle Review of Books* on
March 6, 2017; reprinted with the author's permission.

All photographs shot on 35mm by Nathan Vass,
except for the image on page 205 by Donald Vass.

Originally published in 2018 by Tome Press.